BBC MUSIC GUIDES

———

VIVALDI

D1396191

## BBC MUSIC GUIDES

BBC MUSIC GUIDES

# Vivaldi

MICHAEL TALBOT

BRITISH BROADCASTING CORPORATION

Published by the
British Broadcasting Corporation
35 Marylebone High Street
London W1M 4AA

ISBN 0 563 12856 9

First published 1979

Typeset in Great Britain by
Eta Services (Typesetters) Ltd, Beccles, Suffolk
Printed in England by Whitstable Litho Ltd, Whitstable, Kent

# Contents

## Vivaldi and Venice

Vivaldi is today probably the best known and most admired Venetian composer of all time, if one excludes men like Monteverdi who were born elsewhere but came to work in Venice. He has had his share of luck: if modern audiences had a chance to hear as many chamber cantatas as violin sonatas or as many sacred oratorios as string concertos, they might easily consider Antonio Lotti (1666–1740), Antonio Caldara (c.1671–1736) or Benedetto Marcello (1686–1739) – all natives of Venice contemporary with Vivaldi – to be equal or even superior talents. There is no doubt that many musical connoisseurs of the time thought so. Yet with the advantage of hindsight we can see that Vivaldi fully deserves his pre-eminence, for he chose to channel a large part of his energies into the genre which was to revitalise the music of the late Baroque and spearhead its advance towards the classical style of Haydn and Mozart: the concerto.

Like the symphony fifty years later, the baroque concerto was a repository of form, style, instrumental technique and orchestral devices on which many other genres were able to draw. In extreme cases a concerto movement could be adapted to serve in another context, as we know from Bach's music, but it was usually the concerto style rather than music from an actual composition to which reference was made in works belonging to another genre. Vivaldi himself was, hardly surprisingly, one of the composers most fond of shaping other types of work in the image of concertos, although it is true that he handled certain genres such as the sonata and the cantata with greater respect for tradition than did many other composers of his time. So by revolutionising the concerto and turning what had been a fairly localised vogue for the new form into a continent-wide passion, Vivaldi actually managed to revolutionise the very language of music.

Of course, none of this proves that Vivaldi was as good a composer as he was a historically important one, for the degree of influence composers exerted in their lifetime often corresponds poorly to their significance for us today, as the examples of Lully and Domenico Scarlatti (in their opposite ways) show. Our response to the music, guided by an awareness of its conventions and intentions, is the only proper basis of judgement in such questions of artistic merit. The point needs to be stressed, for until recently most studies of Vivaldi have tended to see him as most significant *artistically* where he was most significant *historically* – as a composer of concertos. Taking a different view, I shall be arguing that he is often at his best either where he is firmly traditional or (paradoxically) so original as to be inimitable. Seen as a provider of concertos pure and simple, Vivaldi often comes off second best in a comparison with composers who copied his excellent designs and then applied their special skills to the elaboration of the musical content – with Bach, who enriched the harmony and texture, and increased the thematic concentration, or Leclair, who refined the workmanship of the solo writing without prejudice to virtuosity. Indeed, for that very reason Bach's arrangements for keyboard of Vivaldi's violin concertos have often been preferred to the originals. No: Vivaldi's strength lies far more in the unmistakable personality which he stamps on all his compositions in every genre – a factor which redeems many an otherwise undistinguished work. No doubt he became aware of his own idiosyncrasies early on and like many other great composers paraded them a little too glibly at times. But without these 'vivaldisms' his music would lack its peculiar sense of urgency, of drama, of pathos, of buoyancy – qualities which his contemporaries and successors could not recapture even as they tried to model themselves on him. If memorability is one test of an artist's stature, then Vivaldi's greatness must be acknowledged, although we may still agree with Arthur Hutchings that Vivaldi could be inferior in artistry to a composer (Albinoni, in Hutchings' comparison – but one can think of much better examples) whom he quite overshadowed as an artist.

He was fortunate, too, to grow up and work in Venice, a city whose cultural life was even by Italian standards exceptionally rich and varied. The decline of the Venetian Republic, which had begun with the opening up of the New World and the establishment of sea routes to the Orient (both developments undermining Venice's traditional position as a trading intermediary between East and West), continued unabated in the seventeenth and eighteenth centuries; it was aggravated economically by a fall in the volume of local manufacture for export and politically by a rise in Ottoman power to the East. Nevertheless, the *Serenissima* (as the Venetians proudly styled their republic) still possessed in Vivaldi's lifetime very considerable territories in addition to the tiny archipelago on which its capital stood: a good slice of north-east Italy, including the cities of Bergamo, Brescia, Padua, Treviso, Udine, Verona and Vicenza; and the two provinces of Istria, just south of the Imperial (i.e. Austrian) port of Trieste, and Dalmatia, further down the Adriatic coast of present-day Yugoslavia. Between 1687 and 1718 Venice also held the Peloponnese (or *Morea*), won from the Turks in an uncharacteristically successful military campaign.

The Venetian Republic enjoyed a political security unwarranted by economic or military strength because of her special function in European *Realpolitik* as a buffer state pursuing a policy of strict neutrality in the many-sided conflicts between the maritime nations of north-east Europe, the Ottomans, and the Bourbon, Hapsburg and other great dynasties. So the ostentatious trappings of Venetian statehood were permitted to remain, reassuring the citizens and providing yet another exotic curiosity for the many foreign diplomats, residents and visitors. A noteworthy contribution to state ceremonial was made on feast days by the Basilica of St Mark's (S. Marco), which like all important public institutions in Venice had its affairs minutely regulated by representatives of the 200-odd patrician families, the *nobili veneti*, who constituted the Republic's governing class.

The Basilica had possessed two principal organs from early times; this accident led to the evolution in the sixteenth century of a novel, antiphonal style, in which the spatial separation of two or more *cori* (ensembles, vocal or instrumental) was an essential feature, the sound now emanating from one source, now from the other, and now from both at once. By the beginning of the seventeenth century this idea was being widely imitated elsewhere, and we know from a letter written from Venice in 1739 by Charles De Brosses, an eminent French visitor who became acquainted with Vivaldi and left an engaging pen-portrait of him, that lesser Venetian churches sometimes employed double chorus and orchestra.

After the death in 1690 of Giovanni Legrenzi no significant *Primo Maestro* (i.e. musical director) was found for St Mark's until the appointment in 1736 of Antonio Lotti. Employment at the Basilica was sought as eagerly as ever in the intervening years by young local musicians of promise, but whether because of the artistic mediocrity in comparison with earlier times or the low salaries paid to the rank and file (a deputy organist would earn twelve ducats annually as against 400 for the *Primo Maestro*!), the most talented among them usually soon left.

Opera provided a more glamorous and lucrative, if less secure, source of employment. The number of Venetian theatres available for opera fluctuated, as in any year a given theatre might revert to spoken drama, close down for financial reasons, or be burnt down, but up to half a dozen were normally active during at least the carnival season, which stretched from St Stephen's day (26 December) to Shrove Tuesday and could accommodate two, even three, successive productions in each of them. Unlike other Italian cities famous for their operas such as Rome, Naples and Bologna, Venice could sustain an autumn 'season running from the middle of November to the middle of December and in some years a short spring season coinciding with the Ascension-tide Fair. Finally, during the summer months, when Venetian society was accustomed to spend its *villeggiatura,* or vacation in the country, on the mainland, troupes of singers whose services the capital no longer required were often recruited to bring opera to such fashionable retreats as Vicenza and Verona. Venetian theatres took their names from the city wards in which they were situated, identified by the parish church. The oldest, the teatro S. Cassiano (erected in 1637), was the first opera house in history to be opened to the general public on purchase of a ticket (except for the boxes, which were rented to prominent local families, often from generation to generation). The opera houses were owned by free-spending members of the nobility, singly or in consortium, but their day-to-day management was usually entrusted to impresarios responsible for the choice of librettist and composer and the engagement of singers and players.

The nobility were also accustomed to have small-scale theatrical works performed in their residences and gardens. This kind of work was often described as a *serenata* (the word is cognate with 'serenade' and refers to the *sera,* or evening, during which the performance took place). Serenatas were usually celebratory or eulogistic; many of them were written for performance on the birthday or name-day of the high-ranking person thus honoured.

Private performances of instrumental music were commonly known as 'academies' (*accademie*). The same word was used to denote a kind of literary or musical club more or less restricted to cultivated members of the patrician class, such as the Accademia degli animosi, a society affiliated to the more famous Arcadian Academy of Rome, whose literary canons dominated Italy for most of the eighteenth century. There flourished in this milieu a large number of gifted amateur dramatists, poets and musicians, who were called *dilettanti* (at the time a laudatory epithet). Such were the brothers Alessandro and Benedetto Marcello, who distinguished themselves in both music and letters, and (initially) Tomaso Albinoni (1671–1751), the son of a rich paper manufacturer, whose later career as a full-time musician parallels that of Vivaldi in many respects.

One type of Venetian musical institution had no counterpart elsewhere save in Naples: the *conservatorio*. Venice boasted four state-supported charitable institutions respectively named the Pietà, the Mendicanti, the Incurabili and the Ospedaletto, which existed to support and educate orphaned, illegitimate or abandoned girls. Some of these girls, called at the Pietà *figlie di commun*, received a normal education but others, the *figlie di coro*, applied themselves above all to music. A rigorously selected group of about a dozen older girls, the so-called 'privileged' ones, taught the younger inmates, and a head girl, or *maestra*, acted as a deputy to the *Maestro di coro* or one of the various instrumental or singing masters under him. Regular services with music were held in the chapels of the conservatories, helping to augment both their funds and their public esteem. Foreign visitors such as De Brosses thronged to the novelty of a superb musical performance by a large, well-drilled all-female ensemble. It is a great pity that the remarkable musical training received by these girls (some of whom, like one Anna Maria at the Pietà, were compared with the foremost virtuosi) did not lead to a brilliant musical career in adult life, which was marked out for matrimony or the nunnery. In Naples, whose conservatories were for boys only, some of the most illustrious composers were former inmates.

The prominence of foreigners on these occasions was symptomatic of an interesting change in the nature of Venetian music. In earlier centuries it had functioned chiefly as an accompaniment to ceremonial, religious and social life; now it was becoming a marketable commodity associated far less closely with the daily ritual of its place of origin. A similar change had befallen Venetian painting in the early eighteenth century: Canaletto (a former painter of stage scenery) turned out views of Venice and Rosalba painted portraits mainly to commissions from visitors, who included a high proportion of English men and women on the Grand Tour. Composers were often approached directly by visitors wishing to take home a musical souvenir of their stay. Alternatively, the visitor could enlist the services of a copyist, particularly if the object was a selection of arias from the latest opera. Music still circulated mainly in manuscript; this was especially so in Italy, where the music publishing industry was both technologically backward and commercially lethargic. Whereas music publishers north of the Alps universally adopted *c.*1700 the process of engraving, in which the cursive, compact and easily legible hand of the best copyists could be flawlessly reproduced, their Italian counterparts, including the Venetians Giuseppe Sala and Antonio Bortoli, retained the cumbersome and unsightly method of printing from movable type, essentially unchanged from the sixteenth century. Also, whereas northern publishers often took the initiative in adding to their stock, commissioning composers to supply them with works or acquiring the music at second hand (not infrequently via an Italian publisher, whom no copyright law then protected), and set up a network of retail outlets in cities far afield, the more parochial Italian publishers seem to have been content for the most part to let composers willing to bear the cost of publication come forward; such a policy depended heavily on the generosity of the person of quality to whom the composer hopefully dedicated his work, prefacing it with a fulsome epistle. So it was more a desire for prestige (or perhaps sometimes a need to expose plagiarists!) than the lure of financial gain which led Italian composers to have collections containing twelve (less commonly six) works of similar kind brought out at intervals as *opera* – authentic and definitive versions of their best works.

If Venice could be said to be backward in the field of music publishing (and this must be understood in a strictly relative sense, since within Italy it was second to none), its musical life was otherwise unrivalled in Europe for variety and vitality. It was possible, indeed almost mandatory, for a successful musician to exercise his talents in many quarters at once. Consider the leading personalities in the *Cappella* (musical establishment) of St Mark's around 1710: the *Primo Maestro*, Antonio Biffi, was also the *Maestro* of the Mendicanti; the *Secondo Maestro*, Carlo Francesco Pollarolo, had an arrangement whereby his son Antonio took his place in the *Cappella*, leaving him free to direct music at the Incurabili and compose operas by the dozen; the principal organist, Antonio Lotti, was in addition a prolific composer of operas, while the second organist, Benedetto Vinnacesi, was *Maestro di coro* at the Ospedaletto; the principal violinist, Giorgio Gentili, gave instrumental tuition at the Mendicanti and had several collections of his instrumental music published.

One of Gentili's colleagues among the violinists was Giovanni Battista Vivaldi, who had risen from quite humble origins. He was born c.1655 in Brescia (a town which occupies an honoured place in the early history of violin-making), where his father, Agostino Vivaldi, was a baker. On Agostino's death he moved in 1666 with his mother to Venice. At the time of his marriage to Camilla Calicchio, a tailor's daughter, in 1676 he too was probably working as a baker, since a document quotes his address as *nelli forni* (in the bakery), but other reports have it that he was a barber. By the time Antonio Lucio, the first of six children, was born, however, he must have become a full-time musician, since on Antonio's baptismal certificate, dated 6 May 1678, Giovanni Battista's profession is given as *sonador* (instrumentalist). On 23 April 1685 Giovanni Battista joined the orchestra of St Mark's. Interestingly, he was initially hired under the surname of Rossi. Recalling the sobriquet 'il Prete Rosso' (the red-haired priest) by which Antonio became known, we may speculate whether the striking hair colour was a trait inherited from his father. Two years later Giovanni Battista became a founder-member of the Sovvegno dei musicisti di S. Cecilia, Venice's best known musical fraternity. He was obviously a musician in demand, for the 1713 edition of the *Guida de' forestieri*, a kind of contemporary Baedeker, listed him alongside his more famous son as one of the city's most notable violinists. He was certainly also heavily involved with operatic performance and management; it could well be that *La fedeltà sfortunata*, an opera performed somewhere in Venice in 1688 or 1689 and credited to one G. B. Rossi, was his composition.

Antonio had in fact been born two months before he was baptised – on 4 March 1678. Whether because of a freak earthquake which shook Venice on that day or (more likely) because of the ailment – variously identified as asthma or angina pectoris – which afflicted him from birth, the midwife had to perform an emergency baptism on the spot, believing his life to be in danger. There can be no doubt that this 'tightness in the chest' affected him psychologically as well as physically from then on. His tendency as an adult to vanity, even megalomania, and his pathetic obsession with money matters must have been encouraged by a life spent in the midst of a large (and expensive) entourage, without whose devoted assistance he would have been virtually immobilised. Equally, his intolerance of criticism can be linked with the underlying inferiority complex to which the permanently sick are prone. Perhaps it is also permissible (while remaining aware of the dangers of romanticisation) to see a more human side to his sickness in the feeling of quiet desolation and solitude pervading many of his slow movements, where the mournful, repetitive phrases of the violin soloist seem to represent a man lost in melancholy.

Vivaldi was destined as a boy for the priesthood. Between 18 September 1693, when he was tonsured, and 23 March 1703, when he was finally ordained, he received training from the Fathers of S. Geminiano and those of S. Giovanni in Oleo. Since his home was in the nearby parish of S. Martino, Vivaldi was allowed during this time to live there – not an unprecedented dispensation, and perhaps one dictated by his health. Meanwhile, he studied the violin, presumably under his father, for whom he occasionally deputised at St Mark's. He will have learnt the harpsichord too, though the only report we have of his accompanying on the harpsichord comes from near the end of his life.

Soon after his ordination, perhaps almost immediately, Vivaldi ceased to say Mass and became a simple abbé without pastoral duties. The fact was held against him later (as we shall see), and his plea that his illness prevented him from doing so rings a little hollow coming from the mouth of a concert-giving virtuoso. Yet an apocryphal story that he disappeared for a while into the sacristy when once celebrating Mass in order to compose a fugue may be a fanciful reconstruction of a real incident when his illness actually did compel him to retire. He seems to have remained orthodox in his religious beliefs. The account by the Venetian dramatist Carlo Goldoni of a meeting with Vivaldi in 1735, first published in the introduction to the thirteenth volume of his Comedies (1761) and reproduced with some interesting variations in his Memoirs (1787), has the composer for ever reciting from his breviary during an at first strained discussion of alterations to be made by Goldoni to the libretto of the opera *Griselda*, but whether this was true piety, sham piety, or a convenient form of escapism is unclear. The German lexicographer E. L. Gerber asserted in 1792, perhaps in fanciful embroidery of Goldoni's account, that Vivaldi was extraordinarily bigoted and left his rosary alone only when composing. It may be significant that like Benedetto Marcello, who became something of a religious recluse in later life, Vivaldi headed many of his scores with a cryptic motto: LDBMDA (often written as a monogram). This may possibly stand for 'Laus Deo Beataeque Mariae Deiparae Amen'.

In September 1703, when hardly ordained, Vivaldi joined the staff of the Pietà as *Maestro di violino* (violin master) at the salary of sixty ducats annually – over twice as much as his father was earning at St Mark's. The Pietà's musical director since 1700, Francesco Gasparini, had pressed the Governors for the appointment of teachers of stringed and woodwind instruments, which they had approved with little opposition. In the following year Vivaldi's salary was increased by forty ducats in consideration of his teaching of the *viola inglese* (or *all'inglese*), a family of obsolete six-stringed instruments similar to the viola d'amore in having a set of sympathetic strings below the fingerboard which by vibrating when the principal strings were bowed would colour the sound. He was not required merely to teach: he had to see to the maintenance of the instruments, acquire new ones when necessary, and compose fresh works to be added to the Pietà's repertory. All the conservatories insisted that their musical staff (particularly, of course, the *maestri di coro*) supplied them regularly with new works, perhaps more out of a desire for exclusivity than novelty, for there was no means of preventing a composer from circulating his music once written outside the conservatory walls to his personal gain, but it was possible to ensure that the first performance of a new work took place within. Vivaldi's appointment was renewed annually until February 1709, when a majority of the Governors voted on a second ballot against retaining him. In the light of his future renewed association with the Pietà it is improbable that he had disqualified himself through misconduct, incapacity, or bad relations with his colleagues, although (to anticipate a later bone of contention) he may have absented himself a little too often. It is more likely that he had, paradoxically, been so successful as a teacher that the girls could now run their own affairs for a while, saving the Pietà the expense of his salary. During his lifetime the Pietà never appointed any other violin master, although cello teachers, beginning with the virtuoso Antonio Vandini, were engaged in the 1720s; departing teachers of wind instruments were often not replaced for several years, until the introduction of a new instrument (the transverse flute in the late 1720s, for instance) made a new teacher imperative.

Meanwhile, Vivaldi had begun to make a name for himself as a composer. In 1705 a collection of twelve trio-sonatas by him in the chamber idiom (i.e. with dance movements predominating) was brought out by Sala. (In fact, this edition may be a reprint of an earlier (?1703) edition, particularly as the title-page acknowledges Vivaldi's clerical status but does not mention his post at the Pietà.) There were two strong reasons behind the choice of the trio-sonata genre for his début. Firstly, this combination of two violins and bass (cello and/or keyboard instrument) was enjoying a final flowering in Italy around 1700. Secondly, as the custodian of conservative compositional and instrumental technique, hallowed by the classic examples published by Corelli in the 1680s and 1690s, the trio-sonata was seen as a conventional test of a musician's ability. Of Vivaldi's Venetian contemporaries already mentioned Vinnacesi (1687), Caldara (1693), Albinoni (1694) and Gentili (1701) all first appeared in print with trio-sonatas.

His next published opus, a set of violin sonatas, was prompted by a visit to Venice by Frederick IV, King of Denmark and Norway. On 30 December 1708, the day after his arrival in Venice, the King attended a service at the Pietà directed not by Gasparini, who was probably busying himself with a new opera at S. Cassiano, but by a man it is not hard to identify as Vivaldi. Before the King's departure on 6 March 1709 Vivaldi had rushed the sonatas through Bortoli's presses and dedicated them to the monarch. No one thought badly of eighteenth-century musicians for such overtly opportunistic conduct: it was the very condition of their survival.

It is fairly certain that Vivaldi had begun to write concertos by this time, as copies of some cello concertos made by the young German musician Franz Horneck on a visit to Venice during the carnival of 1708–9 have survived in the library of the Counts of Schönborn at Wiesentheid, West Germany. It is possible, but as yet unproven, that J. S. Bach in distant Weimar had already obtained manuscripts of some concertos, later to be published in Opp. 3, 4 and 7, and was beginning to emulate his distant relative J. G. Walther by transcribing them for organ and harpsichord. But nothing could diminish the huge impact made on its publication in late 1711 by *L'estro armonico* (the harmonic œstrus, or 'rut'!), Op. 3, a set comprising twelve concertos divided equally between works for four solo violins, two solo violins and a single soloist, some with an independent (obbligato) cello part of solo status. They were entrusted to the doyen of north European music publishers, Estienne Roger of Amsterdam, and dedicated, like at least two other *opere terze* (by Albinoni and Gentili), to Ferdinand 'III', the music-loving Grand Prince of Tuscany. (As Ferdinand did not live long enough to succeed his father Cosimo de' Medici as Grand Duke, the 'III' was honorific.) In a preface to the collection Vivaldi compared Roger's elegant handiwork favourably with that of his earlier publishers, marred by disfigurements, but a more pertinent reason for the switch to Roger, undertaken after *c*.1710 by all the major Italian composers, was an awareness of the greater size of the market for published music in Roger's territory, which stretched from London to Berlin.

A discussion of the style and form of these epoch-making concertos belongs to another chapter. Suffice it to say here that no musical collection published during the entire eighteenth century called forth a greater resonance. Largely submerging notions of the concerto derived from Vivaldi's predecessors in the field, notably Corelli and Torelli, all Europe enthusiastically submitted to its influence. German composers, of whom several resided in Venice for long periods during the 1710s, some becoming Vivaldi's pupils, took extremely quickly to the new idiom and started reproducing it. They were followed by the French and the English (who harboured, nevertheless, a lingering affection for Corelli's ways). The reaction of the Italians was complex. Some of the older, better-established men like Albinoni and Alessandro Marcello appropriated more of the style than the form from Vivaldi's concertos, in effect hybridising them with older models. Others, like the Bolognese composer G. M. Alberti (1685–1751), immediately became more Vivaldian (in the sense of following set patterns) than even the master himself.

Soon afterwards Vivaldi published twelve more concertos, this time all with a single violin soloist, entitled *La stravaganza* (extravagance). Venetians – particularly the sophisticates belonging to academies – had a particular liking for musical extremism of any kind, as expressed, for example, in unusual key or time signatures and bizarre modulations. *Stravaganza* and *bizzarria* are terms frequently encountered in this connection. Accordingly, several (but by no means all) of the *Stravaganza* concertos display a conscious adventurousness. They were dedicated to Vivaldi's former pupil Vettor Delfino (or Dolfin, to take the Venetian rather than Tuscan form of the surname), a member of one of Venice's most illustrious families.

In September 1711 a vote by the Pietà's Governors secured Vivaldi's reappointment in his old post. He held the position against steadily mounting opposition year by year until March 1716, when once again he failed to obtain the necessary majority of two thirds. Before then an unexpected opportunity had come his way. In April 1713 Gasparini departed, ostensibly on sick leave but in reality for good. No satisfactory replacement was found for some years, and Vivaldi thus accidentally acquired the responsibility for composing new works for the chapel. The duties of the *Maestro di coro*, as laid down in 1710, included the composition of at least two Masses and two sequences of Vespers psalms per year (for performance at Easter and on 2 July, day of the Visitation of the Blessed Virgin Mary, to whom the Pietà was dedicated), besides a minimum of two motets per month. Vivaldi evidently took his new task seriously, for in June 1715 the Governors awarded him an *ex gratia* payment of fifty ducats in respect of 'an entire Mass, a Vespers, an oratorio [*Moyses Deus Pharaonis*], over thirty motets, and other labours'.

On 30 April 1713 Vivaldi received permission from the Governors to absent himself from Venice for one month. The reason was the performance of his first opera, *Ottone in Villa*, in Vicenza. In view of his father's association with the operatic world it is surprising that he should have taken as long as he did (thirty-five years) to enter it himself – not so long as Rameau, to be sure, who was an incredible fifty years before his first opera reached the stage, but over ten years longer than Caldara, Lotti and Albinoni. Blooded at Vicenza, Vivaldi almost immediately attached himself to the Venetian theatre of S. Angelo, becoming its resident composer, musical arranger and impresario. This theatre had been erected in 1676 on land owned by the Marcello and Cappello families, and according to the original contract the site should have reverted to them after seven years. For some reason it did not, although the two families instigated legal proceedings – perhaps a compromise was reached. S. Angelo was a more modestly appointed theatre than most of the others, and entrance there was cheaper. It seems also to have operated on more 'commercial' lines, perhaps because it lacked a dominant noble patron. In the carnival of 1713 the manager reportedly took off an opera by J. D. Heinichen, a young German composer who was repeating Handel's Venetian triumph of three years earlier, after only two performances, intending to substitute a new work by a native. Heinichen's opera was reinstated after a great outcry from the public, although it took a lawsuit to secure him payment.

Vivaldi may have stepped in following this scandal. He wrote the dedication of the libretto of *Rodomonte sdegnato* by M. A. Gasparini (probably a relative of Francesco Gasparini), performed in the carnival of 1714, and composed the music for the next opera, *Orlando finto pazzo*, which opened the autumn season of the same year. The following carnival opened with L. A. Predieri's *Lucio Papirio*, for which Vivaldi once again wrote the libretto's dedication (normally this was the librettist's privilege, unless, as here, an old libretto was being rehashed). The second opera was *Nerone fatto Cesare*, a *pasticcio* whose score was assembled by Vivaldi from music by several composers, he himself contributing twelve arias.

On 4 February 1715 a visiting lawyer and amateur musician from Frankfurt, J. F. A. von Uffenbach, was among the audience at S. Angelo.[1] In his diary he recorded his impression of Vivaldi's playing: 'Towards the end Vivaldi played a solo accompaniment [to an aria?] splendidly, appending a fantasy [cadenza] which really terrified me, for such has not nor ever can be played; he came with his fingers within a mere grass-stalk's breadth of the bridge, so that the bow had no room – and this on all four strings with fugues [imitations] and at incredible speed.' Uffenbach later managed to persuade Vivaldi to play to him in private and obtained manuscripts of ten concertos from him.

On 24 May 1716 Vivaldi was appointed *Maestro de' concerti* (director of instrumental music) at the Pietà, less than two months after losing his post as violin master! Some hard thinking had obviously gone on in the meantime. The change in title meant more than a simple promotion: it symbolised a change in the whole relationship between Vivaldi and the institution. Henceforth he was to be valued not so much as a teacher, but rather as a composer and celebrity who chose to associate himself with the Pietà. Characteristically, Vivaldi had anticipated his elevation by styling himself 'Maestro de' concerti del Pio Ospedale della Pietà di Venezia' in publications as far back as Op. 2 (1709).

---

[1] Contrary to most reports, the opera he saw on that occasion must have been *Lucio Papirio*, notwithstanding his statement that Vivaldi was the opera's composer as well as its 'entrepreneur', since *Nerone fatto Cesare* was passed by the censors only on 12 February.

In November 1716 Vivaldi's most famous *pièce d'occasion*, the oratorio *Juditha triumphans devicta Holofernis barbarie*, was performed at the Pietà. Even more than Handel's *Judas Maccabaeus*, this was a patriotic work in which biblical characters and happenings were intended to be interpreted in the light of current events. The Turks had declared war at the end of 1714 and by 1716 had gained much territory from the Venetians, particularly in the Peloponnese and the Greek islands. In late 1716, however, Venetian resistance began to stiffen; Corfu was successfully defended and an Imperial-led army under Prince Eugene defeated the Turks at Petrovaradin. The character Judith in the oratorio represents Christian Venice, Holofernes the Sultan. Sadly for Vivaldi's fellow-citizens, the events related in the Apocrypha were not mirrored on earth: when the Treaty of Passarowitz was signed in 1718 all Venice had to show for the loss of the Peloponnese were some small gains in Dalmatia.

Vivaldi did not neglect his other fields of activity. In 1716–17 Roger brought out three new collections as Opp. 5–7: a set of six sonatas (four for one violin and continuo, two for the trio combination), a set of six concertos, and one of twelve concertos.[1] The interesting thing about these publications is that they were issued without dedications, which implies that Roger, confident of his sales prospects, commissioned the works from Vivaldi. This procedure was to become quite normal later in the century but as yet was something exceptional. As far as opera was concerned, Vivaldi seems to have severed his entrepreneurial links with S. Angelo after *Nerone*, but he was more active than ever as a composer, supplying the S. Angelo and S. Moisè theatres each with two new scores during 1716–17.

In March 1716 Prince Frederick Augustus of Saxony-Poland, who had already visited Venice in 1712, arrived for a longer stay, bringing with him the chamber musicians of his father's *Kleine Kapelle*. One of these, the virtuoso violinist Georg Pisendel (1687–1755), became Vivaldi's pupil and friend. While in Venice, Pisendel copied many works by Vivaldi, Albinoni and Benedetto Marcello, adapting them freely to suit conditions at Dresden, where the court orchestra was based, or his inclinations as a virtuoso. Albinoni dedicated one, and Vivaldi several, compositions to him; the auto-

[1] Roger editions issued between September 1716 and December 1722 carry the imprint of Estienne's daughter Jeanne, although the father remained head of the firm until his death in 1722.

graphs are preserved today in the Sächsische Landesbibliothek, Dresden. As a result of this visit Dresden became a major centre of the Venetian (and in particular Vivaldian) cult in Germany for many years afterwards.

Vivaldi's name was missing from the list of staff members at the Pietà who came up for reappointment on 24 April 1718. He had recently been invited to Mantua, where he had taken his most recent opera for S. Moisè, *Armida al campo d'Egitto*. The Duchy of Mantua, which bordered on the Veneto (Venice's mainland dominion), had always welcomed musicians from its neighbour. The last of the Gonzaga dukes, Ferdinando Carlo, had been a patron of Albinoni and employed Caldara as his *Maestro di cappella* from 1700 to 1707. At the conclusion of the War of the Spanish Succession Mantua passed to the Austrians, on whose behalf it was governed from 1714 to 1735 by Landgrave (Prince) Philip of Hesse-Darmstadt.[1] During the three years (1718-20) he spent in Mantua Vivaldi composed at least three operas as well as many serenatas and cantatas. He was invested with the rather cumbersome title of 'Maestro di cappella da camera' (meaning that he concerned himself with secular, not sacred, music). This title was a godsend to the composer, who must have felt that his talents were insufficiently rewarded with official appointments; he continued to use it after returning from Mantua – with some justification, as he still supplied the court with music on an occasional basis.

He had barely re-established himself in Venice when he travelled to Rome for the carnival of 1723, during which his *Ercole su'l Termodonte* was staged with great success. He must have returned to Venice by July 1723, when he concluded an interesting agreement with the Pietà. Noting that Vivaldi had supplied two concertos for the feast of the Visitation of the Blessed Virgin Mary, the Governors decided to ask him to provide them with two concertos every month, for which they would pay two sequins (approximately seven ducats). When not in Venice, he was to endeavour to send them by post, and when in Venice, he was to direct three or four rehearsals of the new works. He returned to Rome for the 1724 carnival season. A third carnival season he claimed in his correspondence to have spent in Rome cannot be identified with certainty, but it could not have been that of 1725, when Roman theatres were closed. While in

[1] Philip was never in point of fact a reigning *Landgraf*, as an elder brother succeeded to the title, but in Italy he was universally known as such.

Rome Vivaldi played before the Pope and gained entrance to the circle around Cardinal Ottoboni, Corelli's former patron.

By this time Vivaldi's association with the contralto Anna Giraud (or Girò, Italian style) must have begun. She was probably identical with the 'Annina della Pietà' cited in contemporary accounts, though it remains unclear whether she was actually educated at the Pietà or became linked with it via Vivaldi, whose pupil she was. Goldoni informs us that her father was a wigmaker of French origin, and that her success was due to her attractive appearance and good acting ability, compensating for a rather thin voice. In openly associating with a singer Vivaldi was following a popular practice among Venetian composers of opera, although unlike Albinoni, Lotti and Benedetto Marcello he, as a cleric, had no opportunity to marry her. Scandal attended his relationship with Anna and her sister Paolina, who acted as his nurse. In vain did he plead in a letter of 1737 – how sincerely we may only guess – that he lived in one house (of which he could not forbear to mention, irrelevantly, the annual rent: 200 ducats!), while the Giraud sisters occupied another at some distance.

In 1726 he resumed his entrepreneurial role at S. Angelo. Meanwhile, his instrumental works continued their triumphant course. In 1725 his Op. 8, *Il cimento dell'armonia e dell'inventione* (the contest between harmony and invention), was brought out by Le Cène, Roger's successor. This is the collection which opens with The Four Seasons (*Le quattro stagioni*) and includes three other concertos with programmatic titles. Vivaldi dedicated the works to the Bohemian Count Wenzel von Morzin (a relative of Haydn's future patron), whose 'Maestro in Italia' he declared himself to be. From the dedication it emerges that he had been supplying the Count with music – including the 'Seasons' concertos – for some time. On the occasion of the publication of these four works descriptive sonnets ('sonetti dimostrativi') were prefaced to them, and relevant extracts cued into the orchestral parts. Very likely, Vivaldi wrote the poetically rather gauche sonnets himself; that he dabbled in poetry is established by the autograph manuscript of one of his cantatas, in which a recitative text was rewritten in the course of reshaping the music.

In 1727 twelve new concertos entitled *La cetra* (the lyre) appeared from Le Cène. These were dedicated to the Austrian Emperor Charles VI. Vivaldi is known to have visited Vienna from the letter of 1737 already cited, but this is more likely to have occurred later in the decade, after he had met the Emperor during his inspection of the new port of Trieste in the autumn of 1728. A contemporary letter alleges that on this occasion Vivaldi received much money, a golden chain and medallion, and a knighthood from the Emperor (who is supposed to have talked to him more during a fortnight than he was accustomed to talk to his ministers in two years!). A manuscript collection of twelve concertos dated 1728 on the parts and entitled *La cetra* like the published collection (with which, however, it has only one work in common) is possibly a souvenir of this meeting.

In 1729–30 Le Cène brought out in quick succession a final three sets of concertos as Opp. 10–12, this time expressly at his own expense. Opp. 11 and 12 (really a single set) contain a total of twelve violin concertos.[1] Op. 10 was the first set of concertos for solo flute and strings ever published, although six concertos in Vivaldi's style for five flutes and continuo *ad libitum* by the French composer Boismortier had appeared in 1727. Some idea of the novelty, in Italy at any rate, of flute concertos can be gained from the fact that at least half of those in Op. 10 had started life as works for recorder.

No further authentic *opera* were published after Op. 12. An 'Op. 13' (*Il pastor fido*) scored alternatively for musette (bagpipe), vielle (hurdy-gurdy), flute, oboe or violin and continuo, which was published in Paris in 1737, was an ingenious *pasticcio* in which theme-openings taken with one known exception from works published under Vivaldi's name were grafted onto original material by another composer.[2] An 'Op. 14' advertised by the same publisher (J. N. Marchand) apparently never appeared. However, another Parisian publisher, Le Clerc, brought out in 1740 a set of cello sonatas (genuine!) which some writers have confused with this 'Op. 14'.

Vivaldi's reasons for sending no works after Op. 12 to Amsterdam were confided to Edward Holdsworth, an English traveller who met him in 1733, hoping to acquire some concertos for his friend Charles Jennens (best known as Handel's librettist for *Messiah* and other

[1] Op. 12 no. 3 is, exceptionally, a *concerto ripieno* without soloist – the only one of its kind by Vivaldi published in his lifetime.

[2] The opening of a violin concerto in A attributed to Vivaldi in an anthology published *c.*1717 by Roger, but in reality by the German composer Joseph Meck (1690–1758), is used in the second movement of the fourth *Pastor fido* sonata; the finale of the same work is based on the first movement of a concerto by G. M. Alberti.

oratorios), who was an admirer of Vivaldi and had already collected nearly all his published works. In the words of Holdsworth's letter of 13 February to Jennens:

I had this day some discourse with your friend Vivaldi, who told me that he had resolved not to publish any more concertos, because he says it prevents his selling his compositions in MSS, which he thinks will turn more to account; as certainly it would if he finds a good market, for he expects a guinea for every piece. Perhaps you might deal with him if you were here to choose what you like, but I am sure I will not venture to choose for you at that price.[1]

Vivaldi was evidently no stranger to the practice of overcharging tourists, for a guinea was worth over twice as much as the sequin he charged the Pietà!

Between November 1729, when his father sought one year's leave of absence from St Mark's in order to accompany a son (obviously Antonio!) to Germany – to disappear from the record thereafter – and early 1733 Vivaldi travelled widely. Not only may he have visited Vienna, but he very probably also went to Bohemia, where an operatic company led by the Venetian singer Antonio Denzio had been active since 1725 and had already made his music heard at the court of Count Anton von Sporck. At any rate two new operas, *Argippo* and *Alvilda, regina de' Goti*, were staged in Prague in the autumn of 1730 and the summer of 1731 respectively.

During 1733–6 he wrote further operas for S. Angelo and became closely associated for the first time with the S. Samuele theatre owned by Michiel Grimani and managed by Domenico Lalli, where Goldoni briefly worked as a literary adapter. In August 1735 his old post of *Maestro de' concerti* at the Pietà, commanding a salary of 100 ducats, was restored to him. However, the Governors insisted this time that he remain in Venice, since they wished instrumental tuition again to be an integral part of his duties. Following a familiar pattern, he was voted off the staff on 28 March 1738, no doubt having resumed his old itinerant ways. One well-attested journey that he undertook in these years was to Amsterdam, where on 7 January 1738 he directed the musical performances in celebration of the centenary of the Schouwburg theatre, to which he contributed a concerto.

The focus of Vivaldi's operatic activity shifted in the later part of the decade to the mainland, where he promoted many operas, often

[1] The Jennens–Holdsworth correspondence, the existence of which has only recently become generally known, is owned by Mr Gerald Coke.

adaptations of works first staged in Venice. As resident opera companies were usually non-existent, he had to recruit singers and finance the enterprise himself – a task he evidently welcomed. One centre which attracted him was Ferrara, a city just outside the Veneto and under Papal administration. Vivaldi had got to know the Marquis Guido Bentivoglio d' Aragona, who wielded influence over the local opera house, and over a period of three years (1736–9) sought the Marquis's patronage in his efforts to perform opera in Ferrara. We are fortunate to possess much of the correspondence between Vivaldi and Bentivoglio, which is all the more precious for providing the only letters by Vivaldi (apart from dedications) to have survived – ironically, in view of his claim (letter of 16 November 1737 to Bentivoglio) to be corresponding with nine 'high princes' and sending letters throughout Europe. Six of Vivaldi's letters were published as long ago as 1871 by F. Stefani; two more were brought to light by Vatielli and Pincherle respectively, and more recently Adriano Cavicchi unearthed a further five in the State Archives of Ferrara, together with letters to Bentivoglio by other persons mentioned in the correspondence and copies of six of the Marquis's replies to Vivaldi.

In a lost letter of 20 October 1736 Vivaldi proposed to Bentivoglio the idea of mounting an operatic season in Ferrara. Bentivoglio sent an impresario to Vivaldi, who agreed with him to supply two refurbished operas ('which will appear to have been composed specially') at the truly bargain price of six sequins apiece. On 26 December Vivaldi wrote to Bentivoglio, enquiring how the first opera (*Demetrio*), which was to open on that evening, had fared and sending a small change in the libretto of the second (*Alessandro nelle Indie*) for the Marquis's approval. Bentivoglio's cautiously brief reply made no mention of *Demetrio* but endorsed the alteration. Then on 29 December Vivaldi dropped his bombshell. He informed the Marquis that the two operas performed were substitutes forced upon him by the Ferrarese theatre management, after the original agreement had specified *Ginevra* and *L'Olimpiade*. As a result of the unforeseen expenses incurred six sequins and twenty *lire* were still owed to him by the impresario. The rest of the correspondence for that season was characterised by some unseemly arm-twisting by Vivaldi in his eventually successful quest for payment. The whole affair seems to have been rather stage-managed by Vivaldi, despite his acting the injured party.

On 3 May 1737 Vivaldi wrote to Bentivoglio from Verona, telling him of the huge success of his *Catone in Utica* there and proposing another season of his operas, which he himself would finance, at Ferrara. Bentivoglio in reply tried to dissuade him, but must have eventually been won over, for Vivaldi wrote to him again on 6 November about certain difficulties concerning a female dancer who had recently eloped and might not be available for rehearsals in Ferrara at the beginning of December, stating his intention of leaving for Ferrara towards 15 November. Then Vivaldi received a bombshell in his turn. Tommaso Ruffo, Archbishop of Ferrara, informed him via the Papal Nuncio in Venice on 16 November that he could not enter Ferrara to direct the opera, citing his relationship with 'La Girò' and refusal to say Mass – both unbecoming of a priest. This interdict was no mere personal grudge, for Ruffo was currently attempting to stiffen clerical discipline in Ferrara and published an edict on the subject in 1738. The notoriously lax Venetian clergy, who imitated their parishioners in wearing masks throughout carnival, cannot have enjoyed his sympathy. Vivaldi's letter of the same day, a real *apologia pro vita sua* in which vanity and self-pity ooze out of every sentence, was a plea for Bentivoglio's assistance in reversing the ban. This the Marquis confessed his powerlessness to do, and Vivaldi, who could not evade his contracts with the singers, had most reluctantly to consign the venture to Ferrarese impresarios in whom he had little confidence.

Tempting fate once more, Vivaldi, profiting from Ruffo's removal from responsibility for the diocese, resolved to try once more. Two operas, *Siroe* and *Farnace*, were scheduled for the 1738–9 carnival at Ferrara. Then an even crueller blow – this time aimed at him as composer instead of cleric – struck him. This is how he opened his letter of 2 January 1739 to Bentivoglio:

If unfortunates are not aided by the most elect among Maecenases [i.e. Bentivoglio], they must indeed surrender to desperation! I will find myself in this miserable state if you, my generous patron of old, do not succour me. My reputation has been assailed in Ferrara to the extent that they are already refusing to put on as the second opera my *Farnace*, specially revised from top to bottom for the company in accordance with the contract with Mauro [the impresario]. My main failing: my recitatives are, they say, vile. With all that my name and reputation stand for all over Europe, and at any rate after composing 94 operas, I cannot tolerate such an annoyance. . . .

From previous reports I understood that Berretta [*Maestro di cappella* at Ferrara Cathedral] was not capable of playing the principal harpsichord, but I was assured by Sig. Acciaioli [a Ferrarese singer] that he was a fine player and an honest man; I subsequently found him to be ignorant and presumptuous. I was told that even in the first rehearsals this fellow had no idea how to accompany the recitatives. Then, to accommodate them to his level of ability and malice, he dared to lay hands on my recitatives, which through his inability to play them and his alterations, became bad.

The fact is that these are the very same recitatives, note for note, I composed in Ancona, on the subject of which I can tell Your Excellency that they were excellently received, particularly in some scenes made up [entirely] of recitatives.

Whatever Berretta's role in this particular episode, Vivaldi was predestined to be the architect of his own disasters! Bentivoglio washed his hands of the affair amid regrets, and there the correspondence ends.

In the autumn of 1739 De Brosses visited Venice. He related the following in a letter of 29 August to M. de Blancey:

Vivaldi made himself one of my intimate friends in order to sell me concertos at a steep price. He partly succeeded, and I too in my aim, which was to hear him and have good musical diversions frequently. He is an old man who composes furiously. I heard him boast of composing a concerto in all its parts more quickly than a copyist could write it out. I found to my great astonishment that he is not as highly esteemed as he deserves to be in this country, where everything has to be fashionable, where his works have been heard for too long, and where last year's music no longer brings in money.

Vivaldi was not too *passé*, however, to enjoy a last, brief Venetian triumph. The Pietà commissioned him to compose and direct three concertos and a sinfonia performed at a concert in honour of the visiting Crown Prince of Saxony-Poland, Frederick Christian, on 21 March 1740. As the Mendicanti and the Incurabili were also to fête the Prince musically, the Pietà's reputation was at stake; by all accounts it surpassed its rivals.

Anna Giraud visited Graz in 1739 and 1740 to sing in the opera. It is uncertain whether Vivaldi accompanied her, but she may well have prepared the ground for his mysterious final journey. On 29 April 1740[1] the Pietà's Governors, learning of his imminent departure, debated whether to purchase a 'certain portion of concertos' from him. The proposal was defeated, but it seems that they relented at the last minute, for on 20 May he was paid for twenty

[1] The date is given as 29 *August* in an article by A. Salvatori written in 1928 and by most later accounts. The earlier date is proposed in a recent book by R. Giazotto; since it occurs in a freshly-compiled chronological list of extracts from the Governors' minute books, its accuracy is more credible.

concertos. By 28 June 1741 Vivaldi had reached Vienna; this is the date on which he signed a receipt acknowledging payment for several works sold to Count Antonio Vinciguerra di Collalto, a nobleman of Venetian extraction who resided in the Bohemian castle of Brtnice (Pilnitz).

Vivaldi's purpose in visiting Vienna may have been to seek favours from the new Emperor Francis Stephen, consort of Maria Theresa, whom he had claimed as a patron (in the Emperor's former capacity as Duke of Lorraine and subsequently Grand Duke of Tuscany) in opera librettos from 1735 onwards. Opera, indeed, may still have been on his mind: *Feraspe* had been produced at S. Angelo as recently as the beginning of 1739, and there is a tiny possibility that a new version of his Mantuan opera *Tito Manlio*, which was passed by the Venetian Censors on 27 January 1739, was staged even later.[1] Death cut his plans short. On 28 July 1741 he breathed his last in a now non-existent house not far from the site of the present opera house belonging to the widow of a saddler named Wahler, the cause of death being given in the necrology of St Stephen's as an 'internal inflammation'. He was accorded a pauper's burial the same day in the nearby Hospital Burial Ground (Spettaler Gottesacker), long since built over.

A moralising Venetian chronicler recorded the event in these words: 'The abbé Don Antonio Vivaldi, an excellent violinist called The Red Priest and a highly-esteemed composer of concertos, earned in his time 50,000 ducats [annually?], but because of immoderate prodigality died a pauper in Vienna.'

The same words might with little alteration have fitted a more famous composer, who almost exactly fifty years later was also hustled unceremoniously into the grave in the same city.

## Rediscovery of a Master

Although he complained in the dedications of his first and fourth *opera* of unjustified attacks on him by critics (which should have been no surprise, given the novelty of his musical language and the

[1] It is unclear from available information whether the date ought to be interpreted in Venetian style, starting the year on 1 March, which would make 1740 the year of the unlocated performance, actual or intended.

unconventionality with which he conducted his life), Vivaldi publicly received little but praise until the appearance in 1720 of an anonymous satire entitled *Il teatro alla moda* (The Fashionable Theatre), whose author was soon revealed as Benedetto Marcello. Although Marcello intelligently and wittily lampooned widespread abuses perpetrated by Venetian composers, singers, impresarios and their hangers-on, there is no doubt that he had especially in mind Vivaldi and his colleagues at S. Angelo, against whom it has been suggested that he bore a long-standing grudge on account of the legal dispute over the theatre, to which his family was a party. Vivaldi even appears on the title-page in anagrammatic form as *Aldiviva Licante*. Some of Marcello's themes were taken up by others. For example, Goldoni quoted as the opinion of unnamed connoisseurs that Vivaldi lacked contrapuntal ability and set his basses badly – a criticism we shall examine later. Near the end of Vivaldi's life the composer and violin virtuoso Giuseppe Tartini (1692–1770) told De Brosses (perhaps in a spirit of sour grapes) that Vivaldi conformed to the usual rule that a composer who was successful in one style (instrumental) was bound to fail when he ventured into another (operatic). Funnily enough, around the same time the German critic Johann Mattheson commended Vivaldi specifically for his ability to distinguish between suitable instrumental and vocal idioms – a count on which even Bach has been held by some to be deficient! English commentators such as Charles Avison waged a characteristically insular campaign against what they saw as Vivaldi's manifestations of extravagance and freakishness, judging his music from the standpoint of the much staider Corelli and his school. But the very vehemence with which Vivaldi was attacked speaks for his popularity with ordinary musicians, who were well served by editions 'pirated' from Roger by John Walsh and his associates.

On Vivaldi's death both he and his music fell into oblivion. Unlike Bach and Handel, he did not remain in some quarters a 'cult figure' (to use modern parlance). Strangely enough, when the German composers-turned-theorists J. J. Quantz and C. P. E. Bach criticised, not without chauvinism, certain admittedly facile devices popularised by him, they referred to him obliquely as one of 'two famous Lombardic violinists' (the other being Tartini) or 'a certain master in Italy', as if his very name had become unworthy of mention.

When Vivaldi finally emerged from obscurity it was as an incidental occurrence in the grand progress of the Bach revival. Already in 1802 Bach's pioneer biographer J. N. Forkel, probably drawing on the oral tradition of the Bach family, recorded how the great Johann Sebastian, having heard Vivaldi's concertos often praised, not only studied their thematic treatment, schemes of modulation and forms, but also arranged several of them for keyboard. We know today that Bach's concern was not exclusively with Vivaldi: concertos by both Marcellos, Torelli, Telemann and Johann Ernst of Saxe-Weimar (the nephew of Bach's patron) were also transcribed. The first Bach scholars, misled by ambiguities or inaccuracies in the manuscripts and pardonably ignorant of the Italian originals, committed many errors of attribution both to the gain and loss of Vivaldi, but today ten concerto transcriptions (three for organ or pedal-harpsichord, six for harpsichord or organ manuals and one for four harpsichords with string orchestra) can be identified with certainty as based on works by him:

| RV no. | Op. no. | Original Key | BWV no. | Key of Transcription | Scoring of Transcription |
|--------|---------|--------------|---------|----------------------|--------------------------|
| 208 | (VII, 11) | D | 594 | C | organ |
| 230 | III, 9 | D | 972 | D | h'chord |
| 265 | III, 12 | E | 976 | C | h'chord |
| 299 | VII, 8 | G | 973 | G | h'chord |
| 310 | III, 3 | G | 978 | F | h'chord |
| 316 | (IV, 6) | g | 975 | g | h'chord |
| 381 | (IV, 1) | B flat | 980 | G | h'chord |
| 522 | III, 8 | a | 593 | a | organ |
| 565 | III, 11 | d | 596 | d | organ |
| 580 | III, 10 | b | 1065 | a | 4 h'chords and strings |

*Notes*

RV nos are taken from the recent comprehensive catalogue of Vivaldi's works by Peter Ryom (see pp. 37 and 107); BWV nos are those of the *Bach Werke Verzeichnis* (Catalogue of Bach's Works) by Wolfgang Schmieder, in general use since 1949. Where opus numbers have been bracketed, the transcription is based on a manuscript source cognate but not identical with the quoted published work.

On the whole, Bach's arrangements were remarkably faithful. Some of the works are transposed for the player's convenience, and contrapuntal lines are often taken up or down an octave. It must be remembered that whereas writing for strings tolerates – indeed, often benefits in regard to sonority from – wide intervals between more than one pair of adjacent parts, a keyboard can accommodate only one large gap (but this can be really large!), situated between the player's two hands. Even when a pedal-board is available, adjustments of this kind still need to be made. Not by coincidence, two of the concertos Bach arranged for organ were originally for not one but two solo violins: a tough proposition for two hands alone. Similarly, the interweaving of orchestral parts – often irrational or at least confusing when transferred literally to the keyboard – had to be curtailed.

What many early commentators saw as Bach's particular merit, however, was his introduction of changes beyond those forced upon him by the very nature of transcription: his enrichment of the harmony; his addition of thematically relevant counterpoints; his recasting of the string figuration in terms more appropriate to the keyboard; his embellishment of the melodic line (seen notably in the slow movement of R V 316/B W V 975); his occasional suppression or addition of bars – liberties which his mentor Walther also took.[1] These alterations were seized on as evidence of Bach's desire and ability to 'improve' on the originals. Today we can see that losses as well as gains were sustained by Vivaldi's works in their transference to a basically very foreign medium by a composer whose mind worked in a radically different way. In a nutshell, Bach sacrificed Italian incisiveness to German intricacy. We may admire the transformation of the rather plain passage quoted as Ex. 1(a) into Ex. 1(b) (overleaf), but Ex. 2 is quite another matter. At the point marked by the asterisk Bach inserted – perhaps out of sheer force of habit – a semiquaver C sharp (which in transposition becomes B). This note seems to serve a useful purpose as a passing note at first sight, but viewed in the context of the whole phrase is revealed as a blunder. Not only does it destroy the underlying ♪ ♩ rhythm of the first half of that bar, which in the form Vivaldi wrote it has tremendous propulsive energy, but it robs it of its deliberately exact correspondence to the opening of the first bar.

Ex.2   Vivaldi RV 580 (Op. 3 no. 10), last mvt, 1—3

**Allegro**

vns. 1—4

[1] The critics did not take sufficient account of the fact that many passages in Vivaldi's music were kept simple precisely for the purpose of allowing performers to improvise the kind of embellishments Bach and Walther wrote down.

**Ex.1**

**(a)** Vivaldi RV 230 (Op. 3 no. 9), 1st mvt, 48—51

**(Allegro)**

strings + continuo

**(b)** Bach BWV 972, 1st mvt, 48—51

**(Allegro)**

harpsichord

In passing, it should be mentioned that other contemporary musicians made keyboard transcriptions of Vivaldi's concertos. For instance, Manchester Public Libraries possess a manuscript anthology of keyboard music known as Anne Dawson's Book, which contains anonymous but very competent arrangements of four concertos from Op. 3 and eight from Op. 4.

Vivaldi's influence on Bach was profound, immediate and durable. In his more mature works the Italianate exuberance, transparency and frank delight in the spinning out of simple figures of a work like the prelude and Fugue in D B W V 532 for Organ (c.1708) recedes, but the formal precepts and many characteristics of melodic and rhythmic design remained with him to the end. Perhaps the 'Italian' Concerto B W V 971 for two-manual harpsichord, an original keyboard conception that nevertheless comes across as a transcription of an imaginary violin concerto, is his most fitting tribute to the Vivaldi he studied and admired in his younger days.

The first works by Vivaldi to become widely known and appear in modern editions were concertos from the published *opera*, in particular Op. 3. Editors for a long time remained unnecessarily apologetic; the fact that Bach had deigned to arrange the concertos was implicitly seen as a higher recommendation than their reception by modern performers, listeners, and (by now) scholars. For in Germany a book had appeared in which Vivaldi's historical and musical importance was for the first time seriously appraised: Arnold Schering's *Geschichte des Instrumentalkonzerts* (Leipzig, 1905). Fortunately, Schering had access to the manuscripts of over eighty concertos preserved in the Saxon State Library, at this time the only library to possess Vivaldi manuscripts in any quantity. Around the same time the French scholar Marc Pincherle, inspired by hearing a violin concerto attributed to Vivaldi by its performer Fritz Kreisler (who later owned to composing it himself), began his painstaking researches, which were to culminate in his *Antonio Vivaldi et la Musique Instrumentale* (Paris, 1948). A later, abridged version of this work, still regarded as the classic study of Vivaldi's life and music, has appeared in English translation as *Vivaldi, Genius of the Baroque* (New York, 1957).

The delay in the appearance of Pincherle's book was partly due to an extraordinary discovery, or rather two extraordinary discoveries, made in the 1920s, which resulted in the crediting of several hundred new works to Vivaldi's name. In 1926 Alberto Gentili, a music historian attached to Turin University, was called in by the National Library of Turin to investigate the contents of a music library shortly to be put up for sale by the Salesian monks of the Collegio S. Carlo in Monferrat. Excited to find that fourteen of the 97 volumes in the collection contained almost exclusively works by Vivaldi, Gentili endeavoured to obtain the collection for the Turin library, which was accomplished in the following year with the generous assistance of Roberto Foa, a local magnate, after whose late son it was named.

Discovering on close examination of the volumes that they constituted only half of the original collection, which must therefore at some stage have been divided, very probably at the death of its owner, Gentili traced the provenance of the Foà manuscripts back to a Marquis Marcello Durazzo, the son of whose brother, Giuseppe Maria Durazzo, was still living. By incredibly good fortune Durazzo was found indeed to possess the complementary volumes, and in 1930 they were acquired by the Turin library with the assistance of another local magnate, Filippo Giordano, who, by a strange coincidence, had also lost a son after whom the new collection could be named.

The newly-acquired music startled even more by its variety than its sheer quantity. Scores of seventeen complete operas and three larger fragments gave musicians their first opportunity to become acquainted with this side of Vivaldi's creativity, and if the cantatas attracted less attention this was not through any lack of examples. Vivaldi's *musica sacra* was no less a revelation, confirming for many that his attachment to religion was more than skin-deep. Even the concertos held many surprises, for whereas those previously known from the published *opera* and the Dresden manuscripts were with few exceptions scored for one or more violins and strings, here were concertos in abundance for bassoon, cello, viola d'amore, mandolin and many other unexpected instruments, either singly or in combination.

The Vivaldi renaissance, still in progress today, took off from that point. To record a few landmarks: in 1938 a Centre of Vivaldian Studies under the patronage of Count Guido Chigi Saracini was set up in Siena, sponsoring during 1939 a Vivaldi 'Week' which saw the premières of his opera *L'Olimpiade* (with additions from *Dorilla in Tempe*) and four sacred works including the *Stabat Mater* and the well-known *Gloria*; the oratorio *Juditha Triumphans* followed in 1941. Because the concept of historical authenticity in performance was less well developed in those days, all the works were to a greater or lesser extent 'elaborated' in a way generally deemed inadmissible today, but one can say that the enthusiasm of these pioneers made up for their scholarly deficiencies. The war years interrupted the course of the revival, but in 1947 the publishing house of Ricordi inaugurated its collected edition of Vivaldi's instrumental works (*Opere Strumentali*, or OS as we shall call it), of which over 500 volumes have appeared to date. Gramophone recordings of Vivaldi's instrumental music, particularly his concertos, have proliferated ever since. There are signs that the sacred vocal music, which lost some leeway in postwar years, is coming into prominence again.

The time is ripe for an examination of the music, yet it would be premature to do so without first discussing in some detail what musicologists call the *transmission* of the music – the manner in which the composer's musical thoughts have come down to us. Let us return first of all to the Turin manuscripts. Their ownership can be traced back to Count Giacomo Durazzo (1717–94), Intendant of the Vienna Opera (in which capacity he ably assisted Gluck's 'reform' of opera) and Imperial Ambassador in Venice from 1764 to 1784. Durazzo would have had a good opportunity to acquire the manuscripts either in Vienna (where Vivaldi died) or in Venice a little later. The manuscripts of the individual compositions seem to have been acquired loose and in a rather jumbled state; prior to binding in the present volumes they were ordered in rough and ready fashion, so that, for example, the volume known as Foà 29 contains concertos plus an odd sonata, while Foà 28 consists of cantatas, miscellaneous operatic arias and *Juditha triumphans*.

Because several manuscripts refer in one way or another to the Pietà it has commonly been assumed that they represent, collectively, the repertoire of music Vivaldi composed for that institution. However, certain important features of the collection belie this theory. For a start, it includes works in firmly secular genres (operas, serenatas, cantatas), for which the Pietà cannot conceivably have found a use. Then, a high proportion of the works are either autograph or partly so. Since the Pietà employed two girls as copyists, it is notable that their hands are not the most commonly encountered ones. Also, any performing repertoire would have consisted more of sets of parts than of scores, as is here the case. Finally, a large proportion of the autograph works are initial drafts (some of them incomplete and many with drastic revisions) which no self-respecting composer would have let out of his hands.

My belief is that these manuscripts are Vivaldi's private 'reserve' – the ever-growing stock of compositions on which he would draw when called to supply a person or institution with new (or ostensibly new) works. Significantly, most of the manuscripts preserved elsewhere are non-autograph; those among them acquired directly from the composer (as opposed to copied from a manuscript or printed source already in circulation) were usually written out by a professional copyist working from an exemplar supplied by the composer, who then often checked through the copy, making emendations.[1] These copies are often more liberally supplied with marks of expression and bowing than the Turin originals. Cues in the Turin manuscripts show that they often served as exemplars. Opp. 1–12 were presumably prepared from copies derived in this manner, though there is no evidence to prove this.

Vivaldi's circumstances and working methods did not permit him to regard the shape of any composition as definitive. More than Bach and certainly no less than Handel, he constantly adapted his works and uninhibitedly borrowed material for old works when writing new ones, without respect for genre. For example, the *Concerto madrigalesco* for strings (RV 129) is based on material from the *Kyrie* for double chorus and orchestra and the *Magnificat*. To exaggerate a little, he worked on the 'identikit' principle, where the final result is more a matter of recombining pre-existing elements than inventing new ones. For this reason there tend to be wide discrepancies between the musical texts of what is basically the same work preserved in different manuscript or published sources. All the texts may very well be 'authentic' in that they were sanctioned by the composer at one time or another for their respective purposes (publication in an opus, sale to a foreign visitor, performance at the Pietà, etc.), and unless one on principle prefers the oldest version (there is no convincing reason why one should) the decision to opt for one version rather than another when collating the sources has to be made on practical or aesthetic grounds. In fact, the situation is often more vexed, as the degree of concordance between two sources can be so variable, stretching in a continuum between zero and totality, as to make it impossible to decide other than by a fairly arbitrary rule of thumb at what point two variants of a single work become two separate, albeit related, works. The problem is scholas-

---

[1] The volume of twelve violin sonatas in Manchester Public Libraries illustrates the procedure beautifully: their copyist left the title-page blank for Vivaldi to write in the wording he wished; the composer also rectified a number of errors and omissions in the musical text in his own hand.

tic neither for music publishers, who have to decide how many times to issue a 'work', nor for cataloguers, to whom we now turn.

As many readers will already be aware, a multiplicity of would-be Köchels have attempted to list Vivaldi's works in some form of coherent order, making it possible to refer to each of his compositions by a number (or combination of letters and numbers). The most important of these catalogues are those by Pincherle (1948), Antonio Fanna (1955, augmented 1968) and Peter Ryom (1974). While articles have been, and no doubt will continue to be, written about the relative merits of these competing systems, the most important criteria we have to consider are those of completeness, accuracy and rationality. Were completeness the sole criterion, Ryom would win hands down, for it is the only one of the three to include all Vivaldi's works, vocal as well as instrumental. Unlike Fanna, it includes incompletely preserved works. It is also the most up-to-date, for works discovered as recently as 1973 have been included.[1] Enjoying the natural advantage of its later appearance, it is also the most free from simple error. Its supreme virtue, however, lies in the rationality with which it has been organised, particularly in respect of the difficulties outlined above. Whereas Pincherle will identify two sources as one work on the basis of a common incipit for the first movement, Ryom will delve into the entire composition to determine, according to clearly-stated principles, whether the degree of concordance justifies the issuing of one number or more.

So the numbers of Ryom's *Verzeichnis der Werke Antonio Vivaldis* (Leipzig, 1974) with their 'R V' prefix will be used throughout this book. These will be supplemented as appropriate by original opus numbers and the volume numbers (prefaced by 'os') of Ricordi's collected edition.

And so to the music.

## The Concertos

Those who know Vivaldi's music well will easily see the cruel

[1] Unfortunately, the main series of numbers from 1 to 750 was already complete and in practical use by the time these new works had to be added, so that they start, as a kind of addendum, at the number 751. Works of suspected or proven unauthenticity are prefaced by 'Anh.' (short for *Anhang* or Supplement).

absurdity of the oft-repeated jibe that he composed the same concerto hundreds of times over. What is not in dispute, however, is the
fact that he composed concertos by the hundred. Their simple total,
according to Ryom, is 504; if one includes major variants differentiated by an 'a' after the figure, their number climbs to 523; if one
then eliminates lost and incomplete works, the total drops to 494.
When we subdivide them according to their scoring (considering
for the moment only the number, not the type, of solo instruments),
the breakdown is as follows:

| | |
|---|---:|
| Solo concertos | 329 |
| Double concertos | 45 |
| Ensemble concertos (with more than two soloists) | 34 |
| Concertos with double orchestra | 4 |
| Concertos and Sinfonias for string orchestra without soloist | 60 |
| Chamber concertos (without orchestra) | 22 |
| | 494 |

It is useful to begin a discussion of Vivaldi's concertos with some
remarks on the ancestry and early history of the genre, paying
especial regard to the problem of finding an appropriate musical
form for it.

Though many and varied have been the methods of achieving the
degree of coherence in a movement or work which we commonly
refer to as musical unity, composers have always recognised it as
their aim. Sometimes, it has arisen almost as a by-product of other
preoccupations: in vocal genres the musical form is often deter-
mined by the meaning or the versification of the words, requiring no
conventions of its own; in contrapuntal music devices like imitation
are capable of welding together a section or even a whole movement
so effectively that no other method of unification is needed; in any
musical language with a relatively small melodic, rhythmic and
harmonic vocabulary consistent adherence to the norms of that
language is a unifying force. For these reasons pre-baroque instrumental music – subservient to vocal music, largely contrapuntal in
texture and stylistically homogeneous – did not need to evolve
designs based on the orderly succession of themes and keys, of which
we normally think today when speaking of 'form'.

The early seventeenth-century sonata and canzona, distant
ancestors of the concerto, resembled a renaissance motet or chanson
in being pieced together from short, contrasting sections which

were each through-composed, lacking a regular restatement, or *reprise*. The fast sections were generally contrapuntal, the slow sections with which they alternated more homophonic. As the century wore on, sections tended to become longer and somewhat fewer in number, until they became what we recognise today as separate movements. Since the imitative sections of the primitive sonata or canzona were often based on related motives (in extreme cases one section might be little more than a paraphrase, in contrasted metre, of another), a 'cyclic' relationship between movements was often preserved in their descendants. It is still occasionally found in sonatas, sinfonias or concertos as late as Vivaldi's, although it would be wrong to regard it there merely as an ancestral vestige and not at the same time as an attempt, conscious or instinctive, to knit the work more firmly together. The openings of the three movements of the concerto RV 163, all based on a descending series of B♭s and Fs, are a particularly striking expression of this type of thematic interrelationship:

Ex.3   RV 163 (OS 9), incipits of the three movements

The frequent substitution of homophonic for contrapuntal writing in the fast movements of the more extrovert type of instrumental work destined for festive occasions gave composers the urgent task of finding a unifying device as effective as imitative counterpoint had been. At first, the technique of *concertato* (like *concerto*, from the Italian *concertare* – to compete in friendly rivalry) served the purpose. *Concertato*, which reproduces in the world of timbre what antiphony achieves in the world of space, is a system of 'playing off' one instrumental or vocal combination against another. In one sense it was a conservative technique, for since it was effective only when the various groups shared thematic material (which would be tossed from one group to the other), it did not encourage the growth of styles peculiarly suited to each instrument. (Perhaps this was no bad thing, for the solo literature of instruments like the violin evinces an almost too rapid move to idiomatic specialisation in the first half of the seventeenth century.) It was soon realised, however, that *concertato* was a less efficient agent of unification than imitative counterpoint – particularly in the longer movements now usual – and around the middle of the century it became common to have a *reprise* of the opening idea towards the end of the movement – a taste of things to come. Another solution, with which we shall be less concerned, was to cast the movement in binary form on the pattern of a dance-movement.

The first major step in the evolution of the concerto from the sonata was undertaken in the second half of the century by a remarkable school of composers attached to the Basilica of S. Petronio in Bologna, whose senior member was Maurizio Cazzati (1622–77). A favourite genre of these Bolognese composers was the sonata (sometimes called sinfonia) for one or more trumpets and strings, which often functioned as a kind of overture to Divine service on festive occasions. The natural trumpet of the baroque period, whose fundamental note was normally either C or D below the bass stave, possessed a limited repertoire of notes: the notes of the first two octaves ($C$–$g$ on the C trumpet) were rarely employed; the third octave (*principale* register) yielded an arpeggio ($c'$–$e'$–$g'$) and the fourth (*clarino* register) a scale beginning diatonically and continuing chromatically ($c''$–$d''$–$e''$–$f$/$f\sharp''$–$g''$–$g\sharp''$–$a''$ etc.). Whether because it found itself so often echoing the trumpet's phrases in *concertato* exchanges or because the *stile tromba* (trumpet style) sounded so effective on instruments whose resonant open strings happened to coincide with important trumpet notes, the string ensemble came to reproduce trumpet mannerisms almost automatically, even when no trumpet was present.[1]

What was the nature of this trumpet style? In melodic matters it firmly endorsed diatonicism – chromaticism was impossible for most trumpeters in a comfortable register. While passage-work

[1] Strong hints of the *stile tromba* are still found in the concertos and sinfonias for strings of Vivaldi and his contemporaries, particularly those written in the keys of C and D. Good examples are R V 110 and 206.

continued to be dominated by movement in seconds and thirds (passage-work in the 'arpeggiated' manner did not become a common resource of orchestral string writing until nearer the end of the century), the thematically more memorable openings of periods introduced two important new elements: broken-chord figures and repeated notes.[1] The harmony emphasised those chords to which the trumpet could make the greatest contribution: tonic and dominant in the home key, tonic and subdominant in the dominant key. The plan of modulation became fixed by convention: in major keys the dominant was first visited; following an excursion to one or two related minor keys, a triumphant return was made to the home key in time for a final grand peroration. Musical resources missing from the fast movements such as counterpoint, chromaticism and visits to the more distant keys could appear in the slow movements, where the trumpet was accustomed to remain silent.

Side by side with this new type of sonata, the traditional kind for strings and continuo alone continued to flourish. Towards the end of the century there was a fashion for 'heavy' scoring; one or two violas were brought in to lend body to the texture, and where extra players were available parts were doubled to produce an orchestral rather than chamber sound. No sooner had orchestral performance become the norm, than baroque composers, with their ingrained liking for effects of light and shade, began to introduce solo passages. At first this did not entail separate partbooks for the soloists: their colleagues of the rank and file were simply instructed to stay silent during passages marked 'solo' and to re-enter when they saw the cue 'tutti'. One consequence of the reservation of certain passages for solo violinists or cellists was that the solo-tutti distinction could, if the composer wished, reflect different levels of performing ability. Shortly before 1700 sonatas for string orchestra in which the element of display was strong (whether or not soloists were required) became known as 'concertos', the same term having been used earlier for sacred vocal compositions with instrumental accompaniment. It was in this fledgling genre that the stylistic innovations of the trumpet sonata were carried forward, in a synthesis with the new, 'classic' style of string writing established by Corelli (1653–1713) and his emulators.

Corelli himself wrote some of the earliest purely instrumental

[1] A 'period' in a musical movement is equivalent to a sentence in a prose paragraph, its terminal cadence fulfilling the role of the full stop.

works to be described as concertos, although none by him were published until after his death, by which time they must have seemed very old-fashioned to Italians familiar with *L'estro armonico*. It would not be unfair to describe Corelli's *Concerti Grossi* (Grand Concertos), Op. 6, as augmented trio-sonatas with hints of the trumpet sonata and the solo violin sonata thrown in; there is little in them except for their scoring that goes beyond the older genre, and they cannot be placed in the mainstream of concerto development in Italy. If the concerto had a 'father' it was probably, as Quantz suggested, Giuseppe Torelli (1658–1709), who worked in Bologna and Ansbach. Torelli's *Concerti musicali*, Op. 6 (1698), where three of the twelve works contain solo passages, are representative of the authentic concerto in its early stages. The next important collection was Albinoni's *Sinfonie e concerti a cinque*, Op. 2 (1700), in which the six concertos (alternating with six sonatas) have an extra partbook for the orchestral first violins, the soloist playing from the ordinary first violin part; this permitted greater flexibility than when cues alone marked off 'solo' from 'tutti', for now the first violins could accompany the soloist. Albinoni's especial achievement as a composer was the establishment of a vigorous, chordal style with a distinctly theatrical flavour as the one proper for concertos.

Torelli and Albinoni began to tackle the problem of unifying the movement more systematically. Their favourite solution in fast movements (of which there were now commonly two, enclosing a slow movement) was to place a requotable 'motto' at the head of each period, altering its key to suit the context. It was difficult to bring back more than this initial motto, as all the periods except the last, and sometimes also the first, tended to be 'open': that is, they cadenced in a key different from the one in which they started, and so could not simply be reproduced as they stood at a different pitch level without taking the music outside its conventional tonal boundaries.

Vivaldi's great innovation was to make every other period as a rule 'closed', i.e. cadencing in its original key. It then became possible (even if not always desirable) to reproduce the entire opening period substantially unaltered in any of the related keys to which the alternating 'open' periods modulated. This is the secret of the *ritornello* principle. As a result of this step, the soloist, whose rather demure display passages in Torelli's and Albinoni's early concertos were nearly always penned in between the motto and the cadential phrase at the end of the same period, could now be given free rein in the whole of the 'open' periods, which we now style episodes.

The close connection in Vivaldi's concertos between a musical period's tonal characteristics, its mode of scoring and its thematic derivation can be seen from the following tabular analysis of the finale of the concerto for *flautino* (sopranino recorder) RV 443 (OS 105); the first violin line of the opening ritornello, in which five distinct thematic elements (A–E) are present, is appended:

| No. of bars | Tonal centre | Mode of scoring | Thematic derivation |
|---|---|---|---|
| 8½ | C | tutti | ABCDE |
| 9 | C → G | solo | free |
| 6 | G | tutti | ABCE |
| 13 | G → e | solo | free |
| 3 | e | tutti | DE |
| 13 | e → a | solo | free |
| 5 | a | tutti | ABE |
| 12½ | (a) → C | solo | free |
| 6½ | C | tutti | BCDE |

Ex.4   RV 443 (OS 105), 3rd mvt, 1–9

Most outer movements follow the general plan just outlined, although they inevitably deviate from it very often in detail. Some of the concertos in Opp. 3 and 4, which may have been composed many years prior to publication, adumbrate rather than clearly illustrate the ritornello principle. The design is in any case much less standardised than that in most musical forms of comparable historical importance such as sonata form, since the number of ritornellos and the choice and order of keys visited is not laid down. Four or five ritornellos is probably the most common number, and the dominant or relative major key normally the first to be visited, but beyond that it would be unsafe to generalise.

Many concerto movements depart from the model we have been describing in having one or more 'closed' episodes. These sometimes appear at the very start of the movement as a kind of introductory fantasia; good examples are found in the first movements of the concertos RV 565 (Op. 3 no. 11) and RV 249 (Op. 4 no. 8), both in D minor. More often, they are inserted between two ritornellos in the home key, either as the first episode or the last. When two episodes (the first and last) begin in the same key, Vivaldi likes to make them start with the same idea – an effect similar to, and perhaps inspired by, the *da capo* of a vocal aria. Conversely, 'open' ritornellos are often found; they are favoured in the more compressed type of movement (especially in concertos without soloist), since they afford the opportunity of greater tonal variety without increasing dimensions. Vivaldi often achieves great dramatic effect through an unanticipated key shift in mid-ritornello.

The ritornello principle was also adopted for many of his concerto slow movements, but here its presence is often token: the ritornello is miniaturised to the point where it effects no more than a momentary interruption of the soloist's flow; or it appears only twice, as a simple frame surrounding the movement, often ruthlessly abridged on its second appearance.

The other forms used in Vivaldi's concertos must be briefly discussed.

*Binary Form* is used in many slow movements and some finales, particularly those of the lighter type. Both the symmetrical variety, in which the two repeated sections are of approximately equal length, and the asymmetrical variety, in which the longer second section usually manages to requote the opening idea of the movement on regaining the home key, are represented. During the first half of the eighteenth century binary form increasingly encroached on the preserves of other forms, preparing the way for the ascendancy of its descendant, sonata form, in the second half of the century; Vivaldi's music evinces the same trend.

*Unitary (Through-Composed) Form* is normal for the shorter type of slow movement, in which musical coherence is preserved mainly through the use of stereotyped accompanimental figures. Some unitary movements carry this so far as to maintain a ground-bass, either free and modulating as in R V 5 22, the well-known concerto in A minor with two solo violins from Op. 3, or strict and unvaried in key as in the violin concerto R V 172.

*Variation Form*, if the term is applied to movements in which the variations do not lead into one another but start afresh each time, is very rarely found in Vivaldi's concertos, although the Minuet of the oboe concerto R V 447 is a fine example of a species of finale popularised by the next generation of composers. Continuous variations of the Chaconne type, in a stately 3/4, are slightly more common, either as second or third movements.

*Fugue* appears much more often in Vivaldi's music than those critics who have seen him as a prime mover in the 'flight from counterpoint' would sometimes have us believe. In solo concertos the ritornellos often consist of or open with a *fugato* (a set of fugal entries) à la Torelli; a good example is the finale of R V 210, published as Op. 8 no. 11. Even if these cannot be counted as genuine fugues, since fugal technique is subordinated to the ritornello principle, there are plenty of 'pure' examples in the *concerti ripieni*, not to forget the familiar movement in R V 565 (Op. 3 no. 11), a contrapuntal tour de force among the published works which provided useful ammunition for those who in the early days wished to defend Vivaldi against the charge of homophonic frivolity. Vivaldi does not bother with the more recondite devices of the fugal textbook such as augmentation, diminution and inversion of the subject; he does, however, make effective use of invertible counterpoint, stretto (overlapping imitation) and pedal-point.

It was a matter of common agreement among the first composers of concertos that the accompaniment should be lightened during solo passages, enabling the soloist to come through more strongly and also giving him the opportunity for *ad libitum* elaboration without fear of coming into conflict with the other players. One way of doing this, favoured by Albinoni, was to retain all the horizontal 'strands' of the musical fabric (i.e. the full complement of parts) but reduce the number of vertical ones, spacing out the chords. Another way, favoured by Torelli, Vivaldi and the majority of their disciples, was to reduce the number of horizontal strands. At its most radical, this approach resulted in a single-line accompaniment. This line was most often entrusted to the *basso continuo*, a part normally notated in the bass clef which would be played by one or more melody instruments (cello, bassoon etc.) and one or more harmony instruments (harpsichord, organ, archlute etc.), the latter supplying a superstructure of improvised chords which filled out the texture and aided ensemble. Figures above or below the continuo notes, often sparse or non-existent in manuscripts but liberally provided in most published editions, served as a kind of conventional shorthand to guide the accompanist in his choice of chords – hence the term 'figured bass'. A simple continuo accompaniment possessed practical advantages in addition to its musical ones: it was quick to notate and facilitated rehearsal of the soloist's part. (A more dubious advantage in Vivaldi's particular case was that it enabled him to transport material bodily from sonatas to concertos!)

Single-line accompaniments could, however, be laid out in several other ways. They could be entrusted to all the orchestral strings playing in the appropriate octave (the rather misleadingly-named *unisono* accompaniment)—alternatively, to one or both sections of the violins, possibly supported by violas. Such 'basses' (which often momentarily go above the solo part!) were deplored by C. P. E. Bach, who evidently could not tolerate the contradiction of a line that was clearly functioning harmonically as a bass, yet was acoustically an upper part. Occasionally, Vivaldi anticipates a modern, 'pointillistic' style of orchestration by assigning what is essentially a single line to different instruments in rotation – Ex. 5, opposite.

Other typical accompaniments consist of two or three strands, the bass instruments and continuo having been jettisoned. Gently pulsating crotchet or quaver chords in the alto register scored for violins and viola can provide a discreet, rhythmically firm background. Another effective device is to wrap the soloist in a 'halo' of richly harmonised and slowly moving chords in the style of an accompanied recitative, as he does in the slow movement of R V 356 (Op. 3 no. 6). When more elaborate or more fully scored accompaniments occur, they nearly always have independent thematic significance, ceasing by that token to be a mere background; such is the case when Vivaldi introduces reminiscences of the ritornello into an episode. In double, ensemble and chamber concertos it is common for accompanists to be drawn from the ranks of the

Ex.5   RV 237 (OS 325), 2nd mvt, 1—4

soloists themselves. It can easily happen that an ostensibly accompanimental passage in arpeggiated style is at the same time a display passage, as we see in the second and last episodes of the finale to Op. 3 no. 8. Transferred to the keyboard and placed in a lower register, this kind of figuration became the 'Alberti Bass' of the classical era.

One should not leave a discussion of Vivaldi's accompaniments without mentioning his readiness to experiment not only with their layout and articulation but also with their precise tone-colour. To this end he often employs pizzicato and muting effects, rarely seen previously outside opera.[1]

## THE SOLO CONCERTOS

More than three-quarters of Vivaldi's concertos were written for one solo instrument, strings and (with a very few exceptions) continuo. Of the 329 extant solo concertos 220 are for violin. The dominance of this instrument is even more marked in the published collections, as the table shows:

[1] 'Tutti gl'istromenti sordini' (all instruments muted) is a direction which sometimes remains in force for an entire movement or even an entire work, as in the 'Christmas' Concerto RV 270, alternatively known as *Il riposo* (Rest).

| Opus | Year | No. of violin concertos | Other settings |
|------|------|------|------|
| 3 | 1711 | 4 | 3 with 4 solo violins and solo cello (nos 1, 7, 10) |
| | | | 1 with 4 solo violins (no. 4) |
| | | | 2 with 2 solo violins and solo cello (nos 2, 11) |
| | | | 2 with 2 solo violins (nos 5, 8) |
| 4 | c.1714 | 12 | 5 with occasional second solo violin (nos 1, 4, 7, 9, 11) |
| 6 | c.1717 | 6 | |
| 7 | c.1717 | 10 | 2 with solo oboe (nos 1, 7) |
| 8 | 1725 | 12 | 2 alternatively with oboe (nos 9, 12) |
| 9 | 1727 | 11 | 1 with two solo violins (no. 9) |
| 10 | c.1728 | — | All 6 with solo flute |
| 11 | 1729 | 5 | 1 with solo oboe (no. 6)[1] |
| 12 | 1729 | 5 | 1 without soloist (no. 3) |

Another eleven violin concertos, as well as one for oboe and one for two violins, were published separately or in anthologies, probably without the composer's authorisation.

The accompanying strings in manuscript and published concertos alike were disposed as an 'orchestral quartet' comprising parts for two violins (which would frequently play in unison to produce a more massive effect), viola and cello. In published collections Vivaldi and his contemporaries liked to make the cello part 'semi-concertante': it would sometimes diverge from the continuo part to play in a different (usually higher) octave or elaborate the simple continuo line with playful figuration. This luxury was rare in concertos remaining in manuscript, however. Five of the Op. 3 concertos, including one solo concerto (no. 3 – RV 310), have viola parts that often divide, which made it necessary for Roger to engrave two viola partbooks. This is an old-fashioned feature (also seen in Albinoni's Opp. 2 and 5) absent from the rest of his œuvre. A recent suggestion that it has something to do with antiphonal performance is rather wide of the mark.

The character of the writing for solo violin (and, at a less spectacular level, the orchestral violins as well) is very distinctive. In Vivaldi's early concertos, brilliant passage-work is the prerogative of the fast movements, lyricism of the slow movement; but considerable interpenetration of the two styles occurs in his more mature works. His predilection for high positions was legendary; a *c''''* (ninth position) is occasionally found. One concerto, *L'ottavina*

[1] This concerto (RV 460) is an earlier, and perhaps original version of a work previously (!) published as a violin concerto (RV 334) in Op. 9.

(RV 763), derives its nickname from the fact that the soloist has to play all passages marked 'solo' (i.e. the episodes) an octave higher than notated! Étude-like passages, characterised by very extensive use of sequence, are very frequent. It is undeniable that Vivaldi sometimes got so carried away by the technical appeal of such passages – or, to be less kind, by the ease with which they could be set down on paper – that he prolonged sequences unduly, risking to forfeit the listener's interest. In slow tempi it may be possible to salvage the situation by introducing *extempore* embellishment, but in fast movements even the most carefully thought-out variations of articulation and dynamic level do not always avail. Most of Vivaldi's Italian contemporaries were prone to the same fault; they did not have either the discretion or the capability to disguise a harmonic sequence through paraphrase that we see in a Bach.

Much of Vivaldi's bravura writing is designed to extract maximum advantage from the violin's open strings. Whereas a modern string player has inhibitions about using open strings, since they contrast too greatly in sound with stopped strings when *vibrato* is applied, his eighteenth-century forebear, who normally used no *vibrato*, would welcome the fact that an open string freed his fingers for work elsewhere on the fingerboard and could make any interval, however wide, with a stopped note on an adjacent string. This factor explains why the keys of C, D and B flat major predominate among the violin concertos. Open strings are useful for *brisures* (rapidly-broken chords) and double or multiple stopping, which in Vivaldi's music is more often employed for percussive effect than to produce a simulation of more than one instrument. Indeed, Vivaldi on five occasions (RV 243, 343, 348, 391 and 583) brings extra open strings into play by reviving the obsolete technique of *scordatura* (literally: 'mistuning'), in which one or more strings of the solo instrument are tuned to other than the conventional pitches. To decipher the notation of Ex. 6(a) one first needs to know that the strings are tuned *b–d'–a'–d"*. When the soloist then fingers the part as if his instrument were tuned normally (note the two open strings in the forceful *premier coup d'archet* and the emphatic open note concluding the phrase), the sound of Ex. 6(b) results:

**Ex.6**   RV 391 (Op. 9 no. 12), 1st mvt, 1–2

(a)   **Allegro non molto**

Solo vn.

**(b)**

Vivaldi also makes extensive use of a device known as *bariolage*, in which the tone-colours of an open and a stopped note (especially one of the same pitch) are contrasted in juxtaposition. In Ex. 7 notes with descending tails are played on the *A* string; those with ascending tails are played on the open *E* string.

**Ex.7** RV 209 (OS 286), 1st mvt, 48—50

His lyrical writing appears very diverse in notation, partly because he sometimes 'wrote out' the embellishment that at other times would be improvised by the soloist (as in Ex. 9). He is not necessarily consistent within a movement, some parts of which may be fully ornamented, while others are quite plain, lacking even the signs for cadential trills. His melody tends to curve in long, wide arches, in which intervals with a 'yearning' quality – augmented, diminished and compound intervals – are prominent; these help to build up and sustain tension.

For his time Vivaldi must have been unusually sensitive to nuances of tempo, dynamics and string bowing and articulation; at any rate, he took considerable pains to explain his intention as precisely as possible to the performer. Walter Kolneder, the German Vivaldi scholar, has recorded eighteen variations of *Allegro* alone, ranging from *Allegro poco poco* to *Allegro più ch'è possibile*, and thirteen dynamic gradations from *pianissimo* to *fortissimo*. It is legitimate to wonder whether Vivaldi did not sometimes intend a continuous crescendo or diminuendo (anticipating what has been believed to be an innovation of the mid-century Mannheim school) when several progressively louder or softer dynamic levels are prescribed in quick succession. According to De Brosses's report from Venice in 1739, both sudden and gradual changes of dynamic level were then in fashion.

In matters of bowing Vivaldi's imagination and sheer technical flair are unrivalled among his contemporaries and even the next generation of virtuosi. At one moment, he asks the string player to draw the sound smoothly out of the string with long bow strokes (*arcate lunghe*); at another, the player has to produce a series of short stabs 'off the string'. A single bow stroke can take in one note or many, detached or legato in varying degree. In the music of his contemporaries changes of bow direction (which were more clearly articulated than is normal nowadays) nearly always coincide with a new metrical accent; Vivaldi, however, likes to make these changes cut across metrical accents and create a syncopated effect:

Ex.8 RV 763 *(L'ottavina)*, 3rd mvt, 80–85

Several of Vivaldi's violin concertos require a cadenza in one or more movements. Quantz recalled that the practice of including a cadenza arose between 1710 and 1716, and the 'fantasy' Uffenbach heard Vivaldi play in 1715 was probably an early example. In general, the cadenza – to be improvised by the soloist – is not written out, its position just before the end of the movement being indicated by a fermata (⌒) or a direction such as 'qui si ferma a piacimento' (stop here if you wish – i.e., if a cadenza is to be included). About ten written-out cadenzas are preserved in contemporary manuscripts; some of those in Dresden may be by Pisendel, but the rest are by Vivaldi himself. Like ordinary solo episodes (but unlike cadenzas of more recent date) they do not necessarily refer back to the main thematic material; in fact, they go little beyond what one ordinarily finds in concluding episodes, except in being unaccompanied and sometimes including changes of metre. Many final episodes, it is worth noting, end in cadenza fashion with prolonged arpeggios over a pedal bass, often followed by a brief, pathos-laden passage (in which chromatic inflexions or a shift to the parallel key are normal) leading back to the concluding ritornello.

Of Vivaldi's other solo concertos, the most important are the thirty-seven for bassoon and twenty-seven for cello.[1] They are perhaps his 'deepest' solo concertos in a figurative as well as literal sense, possessing a melancholy eloquence that seems to give vent to a *Weltschmerz* only hinted at elsewhere in his music. Not surprisingly, they tend to have comparatively rich accompaniments, with independent motivic interest, on the upper strings. This is a feature paralleled in baroque arias for deep voice; it compensates for the frequent merging of the solo and continuo lines (which occurs particularly at cadences), and lends spaciousness to the texture. The exploitation of exaggeratedly wide leaps, by which Vivaldi often succeeds in giving the impression of a dialogue between a tenor and a bass instrument, is a characteristic of his writing for both instruments.

Some of the cello concertos were undoubtedly written for the girls of the Pietà or their cello masters Antonio Vandini and Bernardo Aliprandi, while others were commissioned from outside. The concertos for bassoon – an extremely rare choice of solo instrument – must have had a more restricted outlet. The autograph concerto RV 502 is headed by the words (later struck out) 'per Gioseppino Biancardi'; a Giuseppe Biancardi born *c*.1700 was a member of the Venetian instrumentalists' guild in 1727. Yet Biancardi was not the sole recipient, for another concerto (RV 496) cites Count Morzin, Vivaldi's Bohemian patron, at the head of its autograph score.

Most of the remaining solo concertos were written for other wind instruments: oboe (19), transverse flute (13), alto recorder (2) and sopranino recorder (3). Concertos for oboe came into vogue in the 1710s. Albinoni published four examples (and the same number for two oboes) in his Op. 7 (1715), and the handful of oboe concertos which Vivaldi included in his published collections from Op. 7 (*c*.1717) onwards obviously swam with the same tide. One concerto (RV 455) is headed 'per Sassonia' (for Saxony). Interestingly, four oboe concertos were adapted from bassoon concertos by the simple expedient of composing new solo sections. The flute concertos were probably written after 1728, when Ignazio Siber was engaged to teach the newfangled transverse flute at the Pietà. Significantly, four

[1] All totals are 'revised' in the manner explained on p. 38.

of the six works making up Op. 10 (*c*.1728) exist in earlier versions, two of which specify recorder (*flauto* as opposed to *flauto traversiere*) instead of flute. Given that the notes *d'*, *d♯'* and *e'* – available to the flute but not to the alto recorder – are little exploited, it is highly likely that several works we know only as flute concertos originated as recorder concertos in versions now lost.[1]

The extent to which Vivaldi models the idiom of his wind instruments on that of the violin stands in remarkable contrast to Albinoni's quasi-vocal handling of the oboe. Nevertheless, Vivaldi was too much of a professional not to make allowance for the special needs of wind players (such as opportunities for breathing) and to omit notes which were impossible to obtain or tonally unsatisfactory on the instruments of his day. And whereas the passage-work is often violin-derived or neutral in style, his more sustained melodic writing is usually well suited to the traditional character of each instrument.

Seven further solo concertos were written for viola d'amore and one for mandolin. The viola d'amore concertos do not differ greatly from the less flamboyant examples of violin concerto except in placing a premium on lyrical expression and occasionally exploiting the six-stringed instrument's ability to descend to a register corresponding to that of the viola's lowest strings. Perhaps these eight concertos were designed to show off the versatility of the Pietà's celebrated Anna Maria, who according to a contemporary report played both instruments in addition to the violin, the cello, the lute, the theorbo and the harpsichord.

Although a great many of Vivaldi's orchestral works, primarily solo concertos, are entitled something more than just 'concerto' or 'sinfonia', very few of them are programmatic. One can discount immediately works mentioning the names of performers and patrons such as Pisendel and Count Morzin or the occasion of their performance (generally a church feast). Other titles merely allude to a technical feature (as in *L'ottavina*) or, more frequently, associate the work with a mood: RV 95 (*La pastorella* – The Shepherdess) and RV 151 (*Concerto alla rustica*) are suitably bucolic in tone, while RV 271 (*L'amoroso* – The Lover) and RV 180 (*Il piacere* – Pleasure) are suffused by an appropriate radiance. The borders of true programme music are approached by a number of works in which sounds of

---

[1] The Ricordi collected edition consistently misidentifies the instrument named in sources as *flauto*, equating it with the modern flute.

nature are reproduced in highly stylised form, of which the most famous is *Il gardellino* (The Goldfinch), R V 90 in its original chamber concerto version and R V 428 as the third of the Op. 10 flute concertos. This leaves seven concertos in which Vivaldi attempts to depict the passage of events: the four 'Seasons' concertos, the two concertos entitled *La notte* (Night), one in two versions, and *La tempesta di mare* (The Storm at Sea), a work surviving in three separate versions.

Programme music was scarcely a novelty in Vivaldi's day, for its origins lie far back in the Middle Ages. However, Vivaldi's programme concertos are among the earliest instrumental works to have a rustic-idyllic content, a pre-romantic feature looking ahead to Haydn's symphonic trilogy *Le matin*, *Le midi* and *Le soir*, and Beethoven's *Pastoral* Symphony. Their influence extends to oratorios, from Telemann's *Die Tageszeiten* (The Times of Day) to Haydn's *The Seasons*. It is noteworthy that human activity (the subject of most earlier programme music) is subsidiary to the forces of nature in all Vivaldi's programme works with the arguable exception of *L'autunno* – a typically eighteenth-century view of the world poised between earlier God-centred and later Man-centred outlooks.

Vivaldi solved the problem of reconciling the programme (which by its nature is non-repetitive) with orthodox musical form (in which the principle of repetition is fundamental) ingeniously and naturally. In outer movements the recurrent portion – the ritornello – represents the unchanging aspects of the chosen subject – for example, the return of spring (*La primavera*, first movement) or the huntsmen's merry pursuit of their quarry (*L'autunno*, last movement). The solo episodes illustrate passing events. Thus in the opening movement of the 'Spring' concerto the following events are depicted in turn:

1. The birds sing joyfully. (Here the two orchestral violin sections are reduced to one player each, and the three solo instruments strike up a dawn chorus based entirely on the notes of the E major chord.)
2. The brooks murmur as they rush along, fanned by a gentle breeze.
3. Thunder and lightning break out.
4. The storm over, the three birds resume their singing (at first a little timorously).
5. The final episode (bars 70–5) bears no caption, but suggests the chirping of a bird.

Whereas in the fast movements contrasted images appear one by one, in the more compressed slow movements they tend to be superimposed on one another to produce a tableau made up of diverse elements. Vivaldi's skill as an orchestrator stands him in good stead here. For example, throughout the 40-bar *Largo* of the same concerto the instruments never deviate from the pattern of the opening, in which the solo violin portrays a sleeping goatherd, orchestral violins the rustling of leaves in the field, and the violas the bark of his faithful dog (which, according to the composer's direction, must be played very loudly and *strappato*).

Ex.9 RV 269 (*La primavera*, Op. 8 no. 1), 2nd mvt, 1–5

## THE OTHER CONCERTOS

As Vivaldi's solo concertos contain most of the elements found in his other concertos, these last can be discussed more briefly.

The *double concertos* include both works for two like instruments (totalling 34) and two unlike ones (11). Most of the concertos in the first group are for two violins (25), but there are also examples for cellos, mandolins, flutes, oboes, trumpets and horns. The relationship of the two soloists is variable; Vivaldi sometimes treats them as an indivisible unit similar to the Corellian *concertino*, pairing them facilely in thirds or sixths or having them engage in close imitation. Elsewhere, the two instruments carry on a dialogue within the solo episodes and are rarely heard together except when one instrument is accompanying the other. The first type of relationship is more common in the concertos for two like wind instruments, the second in the remainder. In the concertos for two unlike instruments the following combinations appear: violin and organ (RV 541, 542, 766, 767); violin and oboe (RV 543, 548); violin and cello (RV 544, 547); viola d'amore and lute (RV 540); oboe and bassoon (RV 545) and violin and cello *all'inglese* (RV 546). Perhaps regrettably, the organ parts in the first four works are hardly to be distinguished from violin parts to which a simple bass has been added: Vivaldi was more interested in the instrument's sound quality than its technical capability.

The *ensemble concertos* are, except for five concertos for four, and one for three, violins, all written for a non-homogeneous group of soloists, in which the instruments, violin excepted, usually appear in pairs. Some of the more exotic instruments required from time to time are clarinets (making one of their earliest orchestral appearances), *salmoè* (probably chalumeaux, ancestors of the clarinet), *tromboni da caccia* (a type of hunting horn?), theorboes and mandolins. In some of the more heavily-scored concertos we arrive at the threshold of modern orchestration, in which instruments are no longer assigned to fixed, restricted functions (e.g. doubling of other instruments) but change their roles as the occasion – or the composer's inspiration – demands. Vivaldi proves himself as amenable as Rameau or Telemann to the doubling, often at one or two octaves' distance, of lines of contrasted timbre; many instances occur in the first movement of the massive concerto RV 558, which has fourteen independent instrumental parts. It is worth noting that a large number of the ensemble concertos are in the keys of C and F major, showing that the intonation of the wind instruments, not the brilliance of the string writing, was the overriding consideration. The three works requiring a pair of clarinets (RV 556, 559, 560) all have slow introductions, a feature associated with solemn church ceremonial, which suggests that the clarinet was used in the Pietà's chapel as a substitute for the trumpet.

The four concertos requiring double orchestra (three with solo violin and one with additional solo instruments) were also intended for religious services. Two of them (R V 581–2) are explicitly 'per la santissima assontione di Maria Vergine'. It must be admitted that Vivaldi's antiphonal effects are rather unenterprising, seen in the context of the great Venetian tradition of polychoral writing. Often the second orchestra is used merely to echo the first or double it at climaxes.

Vivaldi left around sixty concertos and sinfonias scored for string orchestra in four parts plus continuo.[1] Nearly all the sinfonias, numbering approximately sixteen, are in the style of operatic overtures; indeed, most of them were probably written for use in dramatic works, although a few may have been intended as 'concert' sinfonias from the outset. Vivaldi's operatic sinfonias are typical for their time and place: the first movement is always brilliant and open-textured (sometimes with a touch of stridency) and is normally constructed from a series of predominantly 'open' periods which have in common an opening motto and, in less predictable fashion, a certain amount of subsidiary material; the second movement, through-composed or binary, is either a brief link to the finale or, if more extended, an ornate cantilena for the first violins, often doubled by second violins; the finale is a brief binary movement, often with a strong hint of the dance. Two of Vivaldi's sinfonias, however, are of an altogether different variety: the church sinfonia, or *sinfonia da chiesa* – a more fully scored version of the church sonata.[2] Here counterpoint and (in the fast movements) fugue reign supreme.

The concertos, three of them designated by Vivaldi *concerto ripieno*, or concerto for (string) orchestra, amalgamate elements taken from the two forms of sinfonia in proportions varying from work to work. Sometimes theatrical influences are uppermost, sometimes church ones, but most often the two styles coexist happily, producing a corpus of works unrivalled in Vivaldi's output for their marriage of zest and craftsmanship. The opening of the fugal finale to R V 124 illustrates both qualities admirably:

[1] Discounting several sinfonias preserved only in the scores of stage works.

[2] R V 130 is in fact entitled *Suonata al S. Sepolcro*. Like the very similar *Sinfonia al S. Sepolcro* R V 169 it has only two movements.

Ex.10 RV 124 (Op. 12 no. 3), 3rd mvt, 1–13

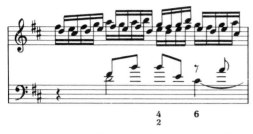

Twelve especially fine ripieno concertos have been preserved as a manuscript set in Paris. Vivaldi seems to have supplied them to a patron (or customer) of French nationality, for the two works (RV 144 and RV 133) that are not also contained among the Turin autographs – and therefore were possibly written specially for inclusion in the set – contain some typical 'French' features: dotted rhythms in abundance and, in the case of RV 114, an imposing chaconne as finale.

Vivaldi's twenty-two extant *chamber concertos* are works for three to six instruments plus continuo. Wind instruments are to the fore: whereas several of the concertos are scored entirely for wind instruments, only one (RV 93/OS 62 for lute and two violins) is without a wind part, unless advantage is taken of certain substitutions (e.g. violin for flute) suggested in the original sources. The bassoon is required in sixteen works, the flute and oboe each in twelve, and the recorder in nine.

In Germany or France such works would doubtless have been called 'sonata' or (following the number of instruments) 'trio', 'quadro' etc., for outside Italy the *medium* tended to determine the title. Inside Italy, however, the main criterion was the *style* of the music. Vivaldi wished to associate these works by virtue of their form and character with his orchestral concertos rather than his stylistically very different sonatas. As similar chamber concertos by his Italian contemporaries are lacking, Vivaldi must be reckoned a pioneer in the transference of the concerto to non-orchestral media. The dating of the chamber concertos is particularly difficult, as none were published. It can be presumed, however, that Vivaldi had begun to write them by the 1720s at the latest, and that the concertos with recorder predate those with flute.

The way in which the ritornello form of the concerto is realised in a non-orchestral context varies considerably. In extreme cases (e.g. RV 107 for flute, oboe, violin and bassoon) the manner of scoring becomes an independent variable, so that the ritornello-episode distinction has to be established by thematic and tonal means alone. At the other extreme one instrument is singled out to play, accompanied by a bass, during the episodes, while the remainder are confined to the ritornellos: a good example of this kind of disguised solo concerto is RV 106, where the flute is the favoured instrument. Most works follow an intermediate course familiar from Bach's chamber concertos – the third and sixth of the 'Brandenburg' set. Here, the full ensemble plays during the ritornellos, while individual instruments (or groups of instruments) appear by turns in the episodes.

Vivaldi's chamber concertos are noteworthy for their exquisite combination of contrasted tone-colours and instrumental idioms. The whole of RV 107 – and especially its chaconne-like finale on a minor version of an extremely popular ground bass also found in Corelli, Couperin and Bach (the first eight bars of the 'Goldberg' Variations) as well as elsewhere in Vivaldi – shows consummate mastery in the way in which it brings now one instrument, now another, into prominence. Sometimes the changes are so rapid that they convey the same sort of fragmentary, pointillistic effect that one often sees in Telemann and the mid-century Germans, and later (in a less mannered form) in the Viennese classics. Modest in performing requirements these works may be – but not in musical substance.

## The Sonatas

If we may discount the *Suonata al S. Sepolcro* mentioned in the previous chapter, Vivaldi's extant sonatas total eighty-two. Nearly half of them (40) are for a single violin and bass, while 'solo' sonatas for other instruments – cello (9), flute (4), recorder (1) and oboe (1) – account for a further fifteen works. Of the twenty-seven trio-sonatas twenty are for the favoured combination of two violins and bass. The violins are replaced by two flutes, two oboes and flute and violin respectively in three further works. Lastly, there are four sonatas written for combinations of a high with a low (or middle-range) instrument in addition to an independent continuo line: two for violin and lute, one for violin and cello and one for recorder and bassoon.

The type of sonata which was identified previously on one hand as the offspring of renaissance polyphonic vocal forms, and on the other as the ancestor of the concerto, was widely known in the seventeenth century as the church sonata, or *sonata da chiesa*, since it was frequently employed during church services and was written in a correspondingly elevated style. As used in the following century, however, the qualification *da chiesa* refers much more to a set of stylistic characteristics than to a place of performance, for most sonatas, especially those that were published and put on sale, could expect to serve much more often as purely recreational music than as adjuncts to a church service.

Side by side with the church sonata there existed a chamber sonata, or *sonata da camera*. Superficially, the chamber sonata in its 'classic' (i.e. Corellian) phase often resembles the 'classic' church sonata in having four movements in a broadly slow-fast-slow-fast pattern, but this is a sign of the incipient convergence of the two types, not a pointer to common origins. In reality, the chamber 'sonata' is a cycle of two, three or occasionally more dance-movements in the same key. In the seventeenth century the various dances making up such a cycle are often so closely related to one another as to be little more than different rhythmic stylisations of one and the same movement, but by Vivaldi's time such overt common derivation rarely persists beyond the first few bars of each movement, if it occurs at all. The term 'sonata' for what is in effect the Italian equivalent of the French (or Franco-German) suite must have been acquired either by analogy with the sonata proper (i.e. the church sonata) or because of the common practice of introducing the dance-movements by an abstract movement sometimes itself called *sonata* in the seventeenth century, although from Corelli onwards the term *preludio* is preferred. (In baroque usage, a cycle of movements often takes its over-all title from that of the opening movement, hence *ouverture* for an orchestral suite of dances headed by an overture proper.)

Five types of dance-movement, all of which are cast in binary form, occur in Vivaldi's sonatas, the great majority of which are wholly or partly written in the chamber idiom. The French form of the name for each dance (better known today than its Italian equivalent) is appended within brackets in the following table:

| Name | Tempo | Time-Signature |
|------|-------|----------------|
| Allemanda (Allemande) | moderate to quick | 4 4 |
| Corrente (Courante) | quick | 3/4, 3/8 or 9/8 (rare) |
| Sarabanda (Sarabande) | variable | 3/4 or 3/8 |
| Giga (Gigue) | quick | 12/8 or 6/8 (rare) |
| Gavotta (Gavotte) | quick | 4/4 or 2/4 |

Vivaldi varies the choice and order of his two or three dance-movements to a degree rarely observable in the chamber sonatas of his Italian contemporaries. It is not uncommon for a *giga* to be the first dance in the cycle – a feature not found in the influential chamber sonatas of Corelli's Opp. 2 and 4 (published in 1685 and 1694) or those of neo-Corellians such as Albinoni, which always give precedence to the more stately *allemanda* or the *corrente*. Although he defers to normal practice in placing the lightweight *gavotta* at the end of the cycle on those occasions when he includes it, Vivaldi can sometimes put the weightiest movement (generally an *allemanda*) last, reversing the general tendency of his time. Unlike Albinoni, however, he never omits the introductory *preludio* – evidence, perhaps, of a reluctance to compose a work consisting entirely of dance-movements.

The coexistence within a single sonata of church and chamber elements, very evident in Vivaldi's mature style, can be perceived in nominal chamber sonatas as early as Corelli's, where occasionally a second slow, abstract movement (similar to that found in a church sonata) is inserted among the dance movements. This affords the composer an opportunity to bring in a contrasting key centre if he so wishes (impossible, naturally, in an opening *preludio*) and to offset the preponderance of moderate or fast tempi in the dances. Further, Vivaldi modifies and diversifies the rhythmic character of the dances, so that sight is all but lost of their connection with the ballroom.

The main agent of church-chamber convergence from the standpoint of the old-style church sonata was the meteoric rise of binary form, which before *c*. 1700 was the property of dance-movements and was relatively uncommon in abstract movements, but between *c*.1700 and *c*.1740 tended to replace unitary form and even made considerable inroads into the province of ritornello form, preparing the ground for the ascendancy of sonata form later on. With the demise of unitary form went a retreat from the more rigorous sorts of contrapuntal writing such as fugue. These two developments removed the principal stylistic distinction between dance and abstract movements, making their differentiation in most cases one of mere nomenclature. Vivaldi's own notable lack of consistency in providing (or not providing) dance titles for movements of works preserved in more than one source attests this rather haphazard state of affairs.

Although solo sonatas dominate Vivaldi's sonata output numerically, and perhaps artistically, it will be useful to open with some remarks on his trio-sonatas, since it was in the trio medium that he made his début in 1705 (or possibly a little earlier, as was suggested on p. 16). The twelve *Suonate da camera a tre*, Op. 1, are of especial interest, since they are his only surviving works fully to merit the label 'immature'. The two general tendencies most characteristic of immaturity are exhibited by turns: Vivaldi's writing is in many places timid and unadventurous, content to trot out well-worn Corellian formulas, but in other places it errs on the side of recklessness; in particular, Vivaldi is apt to over-indulge chromaticism and modulation, where a more sober, purposeful approach as seen in Albinoni's outwardly very similar *Balletti a tre*, Op. 3 (1701), would have been beneficial. Nevertheless, there are many attractive movements – and some inspired moments – in these sonatas. Interestingly, they contain a few fast abstract movements hinting at concerto style, although they are squarely cast in the *da camera* mould otherwise. Perhaps the most rewarding works in Op. 1 are the last two. Sonata XI in B minor (RV 79) features as its third movement a *Giga* which begins in strikingly original fashion: the first violin plays unaccompanied for four bars, 'fading out' with an ostinato phrase whose last two statements are marked *piano* and *più piano*, before the other instruments join in. In the concluding *Gavotta* the repeats are written out with elaborate variations in the first violin part. Sonata XII in D minor (RV 63) is a single-movement work consisting of a set of twenty variations on the popular theme of Spanish origin known as *La Folía*. The most celebrated set of *Folía* variations (the number of sets runs into the dozens!) – and the one to which Vivaldi's version is most clearly indebted in terms of figuration and violinistic technique – is the final work in Corelli's celebrated Op. 5 (1700), his only collection of solo sonatas for violin. Since Vivaldi is free in this sonata to concentrate precisely on that aspect of composition in which he most quickly attained expertise – the idiomatic, virtuosic handling of stringed instruments – its splendid effect is almost a matter of course.

The choice of an accompanying instrument or instruments for these sonatas is a little vexed. Like the great majority of late baroque works – sonatas or cantatas – in *da camera* style, Vivaldi's Op. 1 sonatas, according to their title-page, require an accompaniment consisting of cello (possibly bass viol) *or* harpsichord – not both. Undoubtedly, it was common for both instruments to be employed, since surviving sets of parts quite often (but still only in a minority of cases) include a duplicate bass part, and many contemporary paintings show a cellist or gambist reading over the shoulder of the keyboard player from the same part. However, the very insistence with which C. P. E. Bach, in the Introduction to Part II of his *Essay*, stated that 'the *best* accompaniment ... is a keyboard instrument and a cello [my emphasis]' betrays the true situation during his time. The main argument for including both harpischord and cello in a present-day performance is practical, not historical. Given the instruments and instrumental technique of today, one can rarely omit the harpsichord without sacrificing fullness of texture, cellists having lost the art of adding extra harmony notes to the bass part; nor can one omit the cello without sacrificing power and clarity on the bass line, modern violins being stronger in tone, relative to the harpsichord, than their eighteenth-century ancestors.

Vivaldi had only two further trio-sonatas published – the pair concluding Op. 5 (1716). These are fluent, mature works sharing the general stylistic characteristics of the four solo sonatas which precede them.

His most original trio-sonatas with violins, and without doubt the most mature of the surviving examples, are the set (or fragment of an originally larger set) preserved in autograph manuscript in Turin. The four works are designed to be played optionally as violin duos, omitting the bass, which largely confines itself to the role of a *basso seguente*, simply doubling the lower of the two violin parts (which frequently cross) an octave below. Even when the bass is momentarily independent, Vivaldi takes care not to let it become indispensible to the harmony, as Ex. 11 opposite shows.

The *concertante* treatment, often in dialogue, of the violins and the three-movement plan are very reminiscent of Vivaldi's concertos. Indeed, the choice of binary form in preference to ritornello form for all twelve movements is the only concession to the sonata tradition. Unaccompanied sonatas for a pair of similar instruments came into vogue towards the end of the baroque period, notably in

**Ex.11** RV 71 (OS 17), 2nd mvt, 11—17

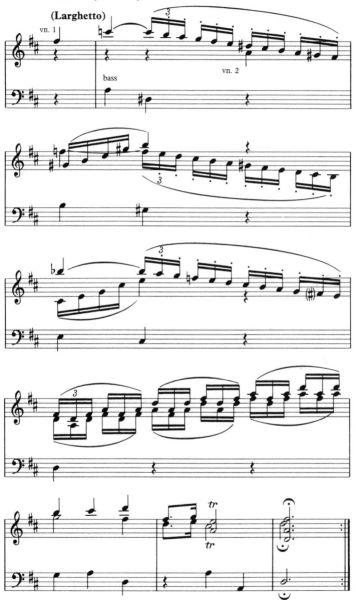

France, where J.-M. Leclair published in 1730 as his Op. 3 a particularly fine set of violin duos showing a great similarity to Vivaldi's examples. It could well be that Vivaldi wrote his four (or more?) works for a French patron or purchaser, and one could easily imagine that they have some connection – as prototypes or as imitations – with the Leclair works.

It might not be fanciful to discern another link with France – this time perhaps a fortuitous one – in the isolated sonata for violin and cello (RV 83/OS 20) and its counterpart for recorder and bassoon (RV 86/OS 18), for French composers were especially fond of combining low with high melody instruments in their trio-sonatas.[1] Both Vivaldi works carry the strong imprint of the concerto, this time to some extent in form as well as style. But for the introductory *Largo* in the wind sonata and the simple continuo basses of both works, one would have difficulty in telling them apart from chamber concertos.

The solo violin sonatas are of particular interest to a study of Vivaldi's evolving style, as the bulk of them are contained in four collections, all of which can be adequately dated:

| *Description* | *Date/provenance* | *Accompaniment* |
|---|---|---|
| Op. 2 (12 sonatas) | 1709, publ. Bortoli, Venice | harpsichord |
| Op. 5 (4 sonatas)[2] | 1716, publ. Roger, Amsterdam | 'basso' |
| 12 sonatas | 1716–17, MSS in Dresden[3] | unspecified |
| 12 sonatas[4] | c.1725, MS volume in Manchester | harpsichord |

Though not explicitly called *sonate da camera*, Vivaldi's Op. 2 sonatas, like those of Op. 1, are all of that type. Similarly, they contain a small admixture of abstract movements in addition to the (for Vivaldi) obligatory *preludio* – two contrapuntal movements entitled *Capriccio* and one entitled *Fantasia*. Their idiom is not over-

[1] This in fact occurs in the movement entitled *Pastorale* from the fourth of the unauthentic *Pastor fido* sonatas attributed to Vivaldi, where the cello part becomes fully independent of the continuo bass. Unlike the Turin works, however, the *Pastorale* has an unmistakably French melodic, harmonic and formal character.

[2] As this opus was issued by Roger as a sequel to Op. 2, its six works (the last two of which are trio-sonatas) are numbered 13–18.

[3] These sonatas are not a set, as they comprise four works dedicated to Pisendel by Vivaldi, seven works copied out (and possibly slightly adapted) by Pisendel, and one further copy by an unknown hand. Nevertheless, they appear sufficiently uniform in style to be assigned as a group to the period of Pisendel's residence in Venice.

[4] The first, second and seventh (RV 3, 12, 6) of the 'Manchester' sonatas are new versions of works found in Dresden.

indebted to Corelli, although the alternation of fast arpeggiations on the violin over a harpsichord pedal note with conventional slow sections in the *Preludio a capriccio* of the second sonata (RV 31) reproduces a formula seen in the *Preludio* of the first sonata in Corelli's Op. 5. In general style they are expansive, even flamboyant in the manner of the Op. 3 concertos, but rhythmically rather unvaried and perhaps a little excessively dominated by motor rhythms. In many of the movements the bass engages in a running dialogue with the violin, sharing its most characteristic thematic material (see Ex. 12, where the bass inverts the violin's scale motive). It is quite possible that some of the sonatas began life as works for violin and cello (without continuo), particularly as that medium was at the height of its popularity around 1700, stimulated by the emergence of the cello as a soloist in the repertoire for strings of the late seventeenth century. Elsewhere in the set, however, busy but thematically unimportant basses point to the harpsichord.

Ex.12 RV 16 (Op. 1 no. 9), *Preludio*, 30–36

The four sonatas published in Amsterdam as Op. 5 strike one as much less expansive, and less self-indulgent. Their form is more compact, and most of the movements (which are all in binary form) introduce a varied reprise of the opening (a feature which later evolved into the recapitulation in sonata form) midway through the second section. By Vivaldi's standards these are 'prudent' works, obviously tailor-made for the conservative north European market.

In contrast, the Dresden works exhibit a more typically Vivaldian, if somewhat unruly, virtuosity. One imagines that Vivaldi allowed Pisendel to copy, or to receive from the composer's hand in token of the two men's friendship, recent drafts which he had not yet had an opportunity to revise and polish. Two works, in D major (RV 10) and G minor (RV 26), are of pure *da chiesa* type; the G-minor work includes one excellent fugal movement in which the violin manages, through extensive double-stopping, to simulate the interweaving of two violins – a device learnt from Corelli. An interesting G-major work in the chamber style (RV 25) has seven short movements, alternately in G minor. Perhaps Vivaldi was trying here to gallicise his style in homage to Pisendel, for works consisting of a large number of short movements in which the tonic – but not the mode – remains constant belong much more to the French tradition and its German offshoots than to the Italian. The bass in these sonatas now tends to have its own distinct thematic character, which is complementary to, but essentially unaffected by, that of the violin. One writer has termed such basses 'unthematic'. This is misleading, for the bass part tends to have a consistency, derived from ostinato-like patterns, which is if anything greater than that of the violin part, since Vivaldi has begun to diversify the violin's material within each movement, breaking up the motor rhythms.

This process is continued in the 'Manchester' sonatas, which are written ostensibly to a rather rigid plan, all being in four movements and *da camera* style, but show an incredible variety of stylisation for each dance. The changes made in the new versions of three sonatas already known from Dresden reveal a continuing stylistic evolution: in the violin part a more cantabile, quasi-operatic line replaces the original energetic semiquavers in a few places; some of the harmony has had its edges smoothed; most surprisingly, the bass has in many movements been completely restyled to become a discreet, perhaps sometimes over-discreet, background.

Without doubt, Vivaldi's most admired and performed chamber

works are the six cello sonatas published in Paris *c*.1740 (see p. 23), which resemble the Manchester violin sonatas in their four-movement plan, though they do not have dance titles. In the entire Italian baroque repertoire of sonatas for cello perhaps only the sonatas of Benedetto Marcello, harmonically and technically less resourceful and far narrower in their range of mood, can stand comparison with these six masterly works, and three other cello sonatas by Vivaldi preserved elsewhere – two in Naples and one in Wiesentheid. Vivaldi's cello has a double character: generally, it confides its utterances to the tenor register and becomes, as it were, a deeper version of the violin; but at other times (and by no means only at cadences) it descends to the bass register, doubling or perhaps slightly elaborating the continuo part. When the two styles of writing alternate rapidly, the resulting intervallic tensions (which are really harmonic tensions compressed into a single line) often recall Bach's sweeping, angular style:

Ex.13 RV 41 (*VI Sonates* no. 2), 2nd mvt, 17–25

(Allegro)

The best of the handful of wind sonatas is the majestic oboe sonata in C minor, RV 53. Vivaldi may have written it for the Dresden oboist J. C. Richter, who came to Venice at the same time as his colleague Pisendel. At any rate the recipient (for whom the oboe concerto RV 455 may also have been intended) must have been an oboist of quite unusual ability to be able to cope with the highly chromatic style Vivaldi adopted. Something of the élan and passion of the work is conveyed by its last ten bars (Ex. 14), a varied restatement or *petite reprise*, of the preceding period. The acridity of augmented and diminished intervals (note especially the diminished fifth immediately followed by an augmented fifth at the end of bars 57 and 59) matches the pungency of the oboe's tone perfectly.

In comparing Vivaldi's sonatas with his concertos we must remember that they were written for the private, unhurried entertainment of connoisseurs, not for spectacular and immediate public effect. Hence they show introvert rather than extrovert qualities, persuading rather than taking by storm. Nevertheless, it would be wrong to differentiate the sonatas from the concertos in regard to style too sharply, if only because so many slow movements from violin and cello sonatas (and some quick movements too!) reappear, hardly altered, in the later concertos. Influenced though he must have been in this by the sheer convenience of taking sonata movements as they stood into his concertos, Vivaldi possibly had higher motives as well: a desire to restore to the concerto some of the intimacy it had lost through its preoccupation with display.

## The Operas and Cantatas

Vivaldi's secular vocal music is dominated by his operas, of which sixteen survive complete in Turin, mostly in autograph. One further score (*La verità in cimento*) lacks merely a final aria; two (*Armida al campo d'Egitto* and *Catone in Utica*) lack one complete act, which Vivaldi probably sent away for copying or rehearsal and never recovered; one (*Il Tigrane*) exists only as a second act, since two other composers, Micheli and Romaldi, contributed the remaining two acts to the performance of 1724 in Rome. These twenty works provide an excellent cross-section of Vivaldi's operatic output, running from his earliest known opera (*Ottone in*

Ex.14 RV 53 (OS 375), 4th mvt, 56—65

*Villa*, 1713) to one of his last (*Catone in Utica*, 1737),[1] and including besides works written for Venetian stages (principally S. Angelo) ones for Florence, Mantua, Rome and Verona.

In any discussion of baroque opera it is important to remember that genuine collaboration between librettist and composer in the sense of mutual consultation and deference to each other's wishes was highly exceptional. An operatic libretto, once completed, was the property of no particular composer: indeed, one measure of the author's success was the number of times his drama was set to music. A libretto was published and criticised as an art-work in its own right quite irrespective of the music it was clothed in. Today we read so many accounts of the inattentiveness of eighteenth-century opera-goers, especially during recitatives, that we are in danger of forgetting that for the literary connoisseurs in the audience the recitatives were probably of greater interest than the arias.

This autonomy of dramatist and musician necessitated the adherence of both to a number of conventions which safeguarded their respective interests. The subject-matter was generally taken from Antiquity, occasionally from the Middle Ages. Particularly in Venice, on the doorstep of the Ottoman Empire, there was a vogue for oriental subjects. Respect for historical fact or the received version of legend was on the whole minimal; however, several librettists of Vivaldi's generation followed the lead of reforming figures such as Apostolo Zeno (1668–1750) and his more famous successor as Caesarean Poet at the Viennese court Pietro Metastasio (1698–1782) in attempting to increase the plausibility of the fiction.

The reformers also sought to restore the unity of action observed in Classical drama and revived in the works of French dramatists such as Racine by eliminating the sub-plots involving comic characters popular in seventeenth-century opera. Banished from *opera seria* the comic scenes paradoxically survived–indeed flourished as never before – as *intermezzi*, generally for no more than two singing parts, sandwiched between the acts of the principal opera (even sometimes in the middle of an act). Pergolesi's *La serva padrona* (1733) is the most famous example, but the genre goes back right to the beginning of the century in Naples and Venice. Having no links with the main work beyond the fortuitous one of being performed together with it, the *intermezzi* often adopted contemporary,

[1] One can hardly count *Rosmira fedele* (1738), a *pasticcio* arranged by Vivaldi from the music of several composers including Handel, Hasse and Pergolesi.

satirical themes, eventually developing into the independent form of *opera buffa*. After a few decades they lost favour and were commonly replaced by ballets, for which we see provision made in Vivaldi's two operas for the 1734 carnival season at S. Angelo: *L'Olimpiade* and an adaptation of *Dorilla in Tempe*. Vivaldi is, incidentally, claimed by a few writers to have written *intermezzi*, but on inconclusive evidence.

Most Italian baroque operas, including all those by Vivaldi that survive, are divided into three acts, each comprising several scenes. A new scene usually begins after the entrance or exit of a character, so their number may easily rise to twenty or more in one act. The number of sets, on the other hand, is much lower – no more than three or four in one act. Since the type of locale (throne-room, temple forecourt, leafy arbour, open countryside, etc.) was highly conventionalised, the same scenery was often used basically unchanged in opera after opera.

The number of characters was tailored to the librettist's expectation of the size of company engaged for the season by an opera house – a size which tended to diminish as the century proceeded and star singers exacted ever more extravagant fees. A common number of principal singers was five, sufficient for two pairs of lovers and a figure of authority such as a king, in addition to which there would be one or two minor roles offering their singers at most a single aria. Knowing that many opera houses could not afford to maintain a chorus, librettists often designed choral numbers in such a way that they could at a pinch be performed by the full cast without extra singers. The balance of the sexes was rarely a problem, however, as half or more of the principal male singers were soprano or alto castrati, who, like their female colleagues, could be relied upon to perform in travesty if required.

An appreciation of the average eighteenth-century libretto requires the modern reader to reconsider the very definition of 'dramatic'. The mainspring of the plot is not the encounter of dissimilar characters but the operation of chance, abetted by mistaken identities and misapprehended words. Human qualities are not the infinitely variable properties of individual characters; rather, these characters are vehicles for a modest range of 'ideal' qualities such as filial piety, martial valour and fidelity in love. Dramatic tension arises less from the interaction of characters in opposition than from the conflict of irreconcilable feelings within a single character.

Moreover, such moments of tension are not prepared over a long time and placed at obviously strategic points; they arise and subside quite suddenly. (One can seldom guess from the text of an aria whereabouts in the opera it occurs.) By modern standards the pace is extremely slow, even if one ignores the arias (which must really be regarded as existing outside the realm of dramatic time, since they are digressions on the states of mind of the characters). What distinguishes an outstanding librettist like Metastasio from the common run is the virtuosity with which he ushers the characters into and out of contrived but not wholly implausible situations and the beauty of his poetic language.

The bulk of the libretto was written in the Italian equivalent of blank verse, usually unrhymed except for a closing couplet. A composer had little option but to set this verse in recitative. The lack of time available to him as well as the need of the cast to commit their parts speedily to memory dictated the choice of *recitativo semplice* (in which continuo alone accompanies the singer) for most ordinary purposes. Strings were reserved for moments of exceptional solemnity or pathos such as a hero's soliloquy. By the time Vivaldi began to write operas practically all solo aria texts (but not necessarily those of duets and ensembles) were constructed in ABA fashion, virtually prescribing a *da capo* form to the composer. The writer knows of very few instances (Clistene's moving aria 'Non so donde viene Quel tenero affetto' from Act III scene 6 of *L'Olimpiade* is one) where Vivaldi abandoned a strict ternary form when setting an ABA text: there he differentiated the two A sections by having the first end in the dominant key, anticipating changes in the aria of the later eighteenth century brought about by the influence of sonata form. In general, musical structure reflected poetic structure. When Vivaldi came, in 1716, to set an old libretto written before the rise to a position of absolute supremacy of *da capo* form – Adriano Morselli's *L'incoronazione di Dario*, first used by Freschi in 1685 – he quite automatically set the numerous short aria verses as through-composed ariettas without artificially imposing a ternary form.

Prudent to the point of unadventurousness in his choice of musical forms, Vivaldi right from the start adopted for his operas a musical language if anything bolder than that of his instrumental works. True, the instrumental composer shines through many pages in his earlier operas. So often the vocal line in arias is composed 'against' a pre-existing orchestral texture in a manner almost prophetic of Wagner: take away the vocal part and you have the music of the introductory ritornello.

Ex.15 RV 738 (*Tito Manlio*, Mantua, 1719), 1/2, 15—22

The thematic (though not the harmonic or colouristic) role of the instruments diminishes somewhat in Vivaldi's later operas, where the accompaniment on upper strings is more likely to be composed 'against' the two-part framework of voice and instrumental bass, and where the orchestral introduction, far from being the germ of the movement, often seems, in compositional terms, an after-thought. The frequent doubling of the voice or the bass in the appropriate octave points to Vivaldi's readiness to follow contemporary fashion and stake everything on the quality of the vocal writing. In Ex. 16 the instrumental parts are thematically amorphous; Cato's grief and rage at his daughter's disloyalty are conveyed by the instruments merely through the use of a bowed tremolo occasionally supplemented by *fp* markings on the first beat of the bar, and abrupt changes of register (e.g. bar 14):

Ex.16 RV 705 (*Catone in Utica*, Verona, 1737) II/11, 11—25

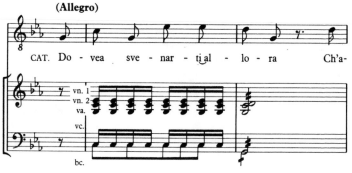

The style of vocal writing also undergoes changes. In Vivaldi's earlier operas for S. Angelo the characteristic qualities are sweetness, pathos, even sometimes humour, perhaps in an attempt to match the unpretentiousness of the theatre. By the 1730s, however, the favoured vocal style is brilliant and rhetorical, as the ten-bar melisma on the syllable 'tar' (of 'spaventar' – to frighten) sung by

Emilia in her aria 'Come invan il mare irato' (As in vain the angry sea) from *Catone* aptly illustrates:

Ex.17 RV 705 *(Catone in Utica)* II/14, 27—36

One final important difference between the arias of the early and late operas concerns the musical relationship between the A and B sections. In the earlier works the use of themes and motives is usually so economical that the B section is content to develop ideas announced at the start of the A section. In the later works, however, the B section is often strongly contrasted not only in thematic derivation but also in tempo or harmonic rhythm. The A section, too, has lost much of its monolithic character. Vivaldi seems to be moving towards the 'polythematic' approach of the Classical period.

Duets, terzets and quartets occur sparsely. The way in which the voices complement one another depends largely on the relationship of their texts. The opening (after a ritornello) of the tender duet ending Act I of *L'Olimpiade* is instructive. To sketch the background: Megacle, the hero, is about to compete in the Olympic Games, in which the hand of his sweetheart Aristea is to be the victor's prize. However, Aristea does not know that Megacle has agreed to enter the Games under the assumed identity of Licida, a friend who once saved his life, so that his victory, ironically, will mean the loss of Aristea to another. The translation reads:

> Meg. In your happy days
> Remember me.
> Ari. Why do you speak to me thus,
> My love, oh why?
> Meg. Be silent, my beautiful sweetheart.
> Ari. Speak, my sweet love.

Ex.18 RV 725 (*L'Olimpiade*, Venice, 1734), I/10, 16—31

Observe how the progressively closer relationship of the two parts mirrors the convergence of the texts (which continues beyond the point at which this extract closes).

The chorus plays a very minor part in Vivaldi's operas for reasons touched upon earlier. Its movements are short and usually in binary form. Often the vocal part, to be sung in unison, is notated on a single stave. The regularity with which Vivaldi simply paraphrased an earlier movement when concluding a new opera with a chorus is some indication of the scant importance he attached to the task. An interesting exception is found in the massive, chaconne-like choral finale to *Il Giustino* (Rome, 1724), in which he sets his four voices in elaborate counterpoint over one of his favourite ground basses; choruses were traditionally an important ingredient of opera in Rome, whose numerous churches could provide the singers.

By the standards of his time Vivaldi was an exceptionally imaginative composer of recitative. A *locus classicus* of his resourcefulness is the dialogue between Aristea and Megacle (*L'Olimpiade*, Act II scene 9), which turns into a monologue half-way through, when Aristea faints on learning that Megacle, victor in the Games, intends to honour his promise to Licida and let him have her as his wife.

The scene opens, conventionally enough, with *recitativo semplice*. However, the violence of the modulations effectively conveys Aristea's mounting indignation up to the point when she falls in a swoon. Megacle's first reaction is one of confused embarrassment, subtly depicted in the accompaniment by halting crotchets separated by long rests to be played by all the strings in unison with the bass. On realising Aristea's condition, Megacle becomes frantic; the strings play four-part detached chords laced with furious arpeggios on the violins which wrench the harmony brutally from one key into another (Ex. 19 overleaf). Finally, Megacle bids Aristea farewell in an *accompagnato* of standard type, in which the strings envelop the singer in slowly-moving chords, the poignancy being enhanced by numerous appoggiaturas in the vocal line.

In his operas – indeed, in his vocal music as a whole – Vivaldi shows himself to be a much better word-*painter* than word-*setter*. His ability to conjure up a mood through the use of particular melodic or rhythmic inflexions, through the texture of the parts or through tone-colour, was remarkable, but he was often inexcusably cavalier in his treatment of the individual word. Licida's aria 'Qual

Ex.19 RV 725 *(L'Olimpiade)*, II/9

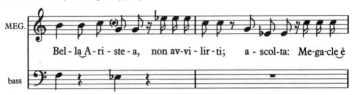

MEG.

Bel - la A - ri - ste - a, non av - vi - lir - ti; a - scol - ta: Me - ga - cle è

bass

(vns. va. *an octave higher*)

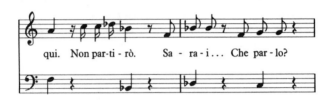

qui. Non par - ti - rò. Sa - ra - i... Che par - lo?

El - la non m'o - de. A - ve - te, o stel - le, più sven-

vn. 1
vn. 2
va.

bass

- tu - re per me?

destrier che all'albergo è vicino' (*L'Olimpiade*, Act I scene 3) shows Vivaldi's strength and weakness well. This is an example of a 'comparison' aria, in which the singer's condition is likened to a phenomenon of the natural world – here, a stallion hastening towards its stable with such impatience that neither its bridle nor the voice of its rider can restrain it. Vivaldi captures the horse's impetuosity marvellously with bowed tremolos in the bass part and bounding rhythms such as ♩ ♪♫ which seem to race towards the bar-line. Trills suggest neighing. The loud voice of the rider is conveyed by declamation on a monotone, reinforced shrilly an octave higher by the violins. The word-setting begins perfectly satisfactorily. It is not long, however, before Vivaldi starts to develop his motives autonomously, as if in an instrumental composition. At this point portions of text are brought back in almost random sequence so that a musical idea designed for one poetic image now sometimes has to accompany another. Nor does Vivaldi shrink from distorting the prosody when it suits him, introducing a hiatus here and an elision there. In fairness to him, it must be admitted that few of his contemporaries were much better.

To assess Vivaldi's discrimination in dramatic matters one need look no further than the adaptations made to the last two acts of the libretto for *Catone in Utica*.[1] Whether he undertook this work of adaptation himself, as the autograph manuscript of the opera suggests, or whether he merely sanctioned alterations made by someone else is of little consequence, so drastic were the implications for the drama. *Catone in Utica*, first set by Vinci in 1727, is one of Metastasio's strongest creations. Its plot can be summarised as follows:

*Act I*
Caesar, having defeated Pompey, has made himself Dictator for life. Only Cato, a Roman senator stubbornly faithful to the Republic, still resists him. In his north African stronghold of Utica Cato enlists the support of Arbace, a Numidian prince, hoping to cement the alliance by giving his daughter Marzia in marriage to him. Marzia, however, is secretly in love with Caesar and presses for a deferment of the wedding. Caesar, who respects Cato and wishes to win him over by persuasion, arrives on a mission of peace. Pompey's widow Emilia, who is set on vengeance, attempts to dissuade Cato from considering Caesar's overtures. Cato retires to consider his position and Caesar returns to his besieging troops, promising to return.
*Act II*
Caesar's envoy Fulvio tries to convince Cato of the futility of resistance by reading

---

[1] The first act is missing from the Turin score.

him a letter from the Senate ordering him to capitulate. Under pressure from Marzia and the populace, Cato reluctantly agrees to see Caesar. Caesar's peace terms are generous but Cato remains implacable. (The argument between the two men on the relative merits of democracy and dictatorship, in scene 10, is remarkably modern in spirit.) War being inevitable, Caesar leaves. Emilia tries to lure him into an ambush by directing him to a secret passage via a complicated ruse involving Fulvio.

*Act III*

Caesar, magnanimously given safe conduct by Arbace, is saved from Emilia's ambush by Cato, who, having uncovered Marzia's disloyalty to him, is pursuing her down the same passage. Fulvio arrives with troops to announce that Utica has fallen to Caesar, whereupon Cato and his party surrender. Stabbing himself in a last, defiant gesture, Cato secures from his repentant daughter a vow of hostility to Caesar and a promise to marry Arbace. Expiring, he prophesies Brutus's assassination of Caesar.

Because the sight of a wounded Cato on stage offended a section of the contemporary public, Metastasio was induced to modify the end of the last act, somewhat weakening its effect and damaging the coherence of the plot. Vivaldi's further modifications were of a different order, however. Firstly, several arias were added, while others were omitted or received new texts – quite normal practice when operas were revived. Secondly, some questionable cuts were made. Much of Act II scene 10 was omitted, depriving the audience of an insight into the reasons for Cato's intransigence. Most seriously, however, Vivaldi altered the ending out of all recognition: Cato is pardoned by Caesar (and graciously accepts the pardon); Arbace renounces his love for Marzia 'for the good of the nation'; Caesar, forswearing worldly ambition, declares his intention of marrying Marzia. One might as well end *Hamlet* with the wedding of the prince to Ophelia under the benign eye of Polonius! No doubt, Vivaldi judged the Veronese public astutely, but we are entitled to regret his lack of a dramatic conscience.

Vivaldi's use of instruments was if anything more imaginative in his operas than in his concertos. The backbone of his orchestra, present in practically every aria, was the string ensemble. By giving the parts contrasting figuration, by doubling or leaving out certain parts (the continuo is often suppressed) and by employing special effects such as pizzicato and muting in all or only some of the parts, he was able to produce highly original sounds without bringing in extra instruments. An almost perverse ingenuity is seen in an aria such as Anastasio's 'Sento in seno ch'in pioggia di lagrime' (I feel in my breast that in a rain of tears) from Act II scene 1 of *Il Giustino,* where all the strings (minus continuo) are directed to play pizzicato in illustration of rain except for one first violin, one second violin and one *violone*, who have to play with their bows. Earlier in the same opera (Act I scene 4) there is an aria in pastorale style (recalling the *Pifa* movement in Handel's *Messiah*), where double basses independently sustain a drone bass *C*. In one aria from *Orlando finto pazzo* (1714) both sections of violins are instructed to play violas in order to evoke the gloom of the nether regions. Caesar's aria 'Se mai senti spirarti sul volto' (If ever you feel wafting in your face) from Act II scene 5 of *Catone* has pizzicato violas doubling the bass tremolando style beneath muted violins.

The only obbligato instruments used with any regularity in Vivaldi's operas are horns, trumpets, recorders and oboes. Nearly every opera has at least one 'hunting' aria in F major with parts for a pair of braying horns. There are two instances where a single horn is used to provide orchestral colour with long pedal notes in the middle of the texture. One is in *L'Olimpiade*; the other, in *Farnace* (1727 and 1739), is remarkable for two reasons: firstly, the key of the aria is not F major but C minor – not until the age of Haydn and Mozart did it become common to employ the horn in a key other than that in which it was pitched; secondly, Vivaldi, probably learning from his experience in the earlier performance, directs in his later score prepared for the thwarted performance at Ferrara that a second horn play alongside the first, drawing breath at different times so that no breaks occur – an even more modern conception!

Trumpets, pitched in C or D and sometimes accompanied by timpani, appear in 'martial' arias and sinfonias, such as the 'Sinfonia per il combattimento' in *Dario*.[1] Recorders and oboes are more versatile, but are especially characteristic of arias in a pastoral vein.

Nearly every opera contains one or two – rarely more – arias in which an unusual obbligato instrument appears as a novelty. Some of the instruments themselves are rarities – the *viola all'inglese* (*Dario*), psaltery (*Il Giustino*) and *flautino* (*Tito Manlio*); others are exceptional only in their context – the harpsichord (*Arsilda*), bassoon (*Dario*), cello (*Tito Manlio*) and tranverse flute (*Orlando furioso*). Since all the operas are precisely datable, the choice of obbligato instruments and the style of writing for them offers many clues for the dating of concertos featuring the same instruments.

[1] Not only the overture to the first act but also any piece of purely instrumental music occurring in an opera can be called 'sinfonia'.

Another interesting point of comparison between operas and concertos which has yet to be explored systematically is the borrowing of material. Vivaldi not only liked to reuse old arias, substituting a new text if necessary, but also drew copiously on his instrumental music throughout his operas. A condensed version in binary form of the opening movement of the 'Spring' concerto is used as a sinfonia, with instruments on the stage, during the first act of *Il Giustino*. The *Tempesta di mare* sinfonia in *La fida ninfa* is based on the opening movement of the concerto of the same name (RV 253). A rescored version of the first movement of the *Concerto funebre* RV 579 is used for the entry of the condemned Manlio in the last act of *Tito Manlio*. Besides these adapted instrumental movements innumerable arias, particularly in their ritornellos, have clear affinities with instrumental works. For instance, each of the three movements of one recorder concerto (RV 442) has relatives within the operatic music: the first movement in an aria from *Il Giustino*, the second in one from *Il Tigrane*, and the last in one from *Il Teuzzone*. In these cases it would sometimes be unwise to discount the possibility that the vocal movement came first.

The disappointing response to staged performances in recent times of *L'Olimpiade, La fida ninfa* and *Griselda* suggests that Vivaldi's operas will be hard to revive successfully in their original form. One way of rescuing their best music while preserving a little of the integrity of the original would be to present in concert performance all the arias for one (or more) of the characters in an opera. Recordings offer another possible route to salvation.

Fortunately, Vivaldi wrote a number of shorter dramatic works (three survive) which might fare better on the stage. These are *serenate*: works commissioned for performance in the evening in celebration of some event or in homage to some illustrious person on his birthday or name-day. The serenata RV 687 written for two allegorical characters, Imeneo (Hymen) and Gloria, was performed, possibly in Venice at the French ambassador's residence, to mark the occasion of Louis XV's marriage to the Polish princess Marie Leczinska on 5 September 1725. RV 693, entitled *La Sena festeggiante* (The Seine rejoicing), is another essay in flattery towards the French monarch. It has been suggested that the work commemorates the birth of the Dauphin in 1729, but it seems more likely that it was composed for a royal birthday. There are hints in the score that the performance took place in Paris: before the appropriate staves at the head of the first ensemble Vivaldi wrote '2 hautbois o più se piace' (2 oboes or more if you like), similarly '2 flauti o più', as if he anticipated that more than four wind players would be available but lacked precise knowledge; even more significantly, the closing ensemble – a transposed version, to new words, of the final chorus of *Il Giustino* – has the following rubric at the head of the tenor part: 'It will be very good if the tenor is sung, but this is not essential'. Evidently, Vivaldi did not know whether the three characters Età dell'oro (The Age of Gold – soprano), Virtù (Virtue – alto) and Sena (The Seine – bass) would be reinforced by a chorus with tenors. In several movements besides this choral chaconne Vivaldi attempts to imitate the French style. Età dell'oro has a pair of minuet-arias, and the second part of the serenata begins with a French overture. Fine as the overture is, a truly French flavour eludes it. For one thing, the fugal entries opening the quick section ascend from the bass, whereas in a conventional French overture they descend from the first violins. Vivaldi was always too much himself to be a faithful imitator.

Two of the Turin volumes and a few scattered sources elsewhere contain cantatas by Vivaldi. These small-scale works are nothing like the church cantatas of Bach, for by 'cantata' the Italians generally meant a setting of specially-composed secular verse for one singer accompanied by continuo (harpsichord and/or cello) and sometimes other instruments. Predictably, the largest group among Vivaldi's cantatas is for soprano and continuo (22), followed by alto and continuo (8), soprano, instrument(s) and continuo (5) and alto, instrument(s) and continuo (4). The absence of works for tenor and bass is mainly to be explained by the fact that a high proportion of the male singers employed at the courts of the nobility, for whom most cantatas were written, were castrati.

Nearly all Vivaldi's cantatas consist of a pair of arias separated, sometimes also introduced, by a recitative. The poetry, in keeping with the prevailing Arcadian conventions of the early eighteenth century, treats of the pleasures and pangs of love among shepherds and nymphs, usually in the form of a soliloquy, though the singer may occasionally assume the function of a narrator for a few lines. The artificiality and triteness of the verse is deplorable. Fortunately, the music makes amends. It is noticeable how expressive in their vocal line (though not so much in the harmony and modulation) Vivaldi's cantata recitatives are, compared with their operatic counterparts. One obvious possible reason is that the former were not designed for memorisation. In his arias Vivaldi likes to set a strongly articulated bass part, in which ostinato patterns are often discernible, against a more fluid, less tightly structured vocal line.

The cantatas with instruments are stylistically indebted to the dramatic works. Two of them, indeed, resemble serenatas in their connection with a particular event. 'O mie porpore più belle' (RV 685) was written for the installation of a new bishop of Mantua in 1719, while 'Qual in pioggia dorata' (RV 686) pays homage (on his birthday?) to the Governor of Mantua, Landgrave Philip, appropriately to the sound of two horns.

# The Sacred Music

It is ironical that Vivaldi, ordained a priest in 1703, did not apparently write any sacred vocal music until an opportunity was provided by Gasparini's sudden departure from the Pietà in the middle of 1713. The duties of the *Maestro di coro*, as we saw, included the regular composition of masses, vespers and motets. A mass would comprise the five sections of the Ordinary (*Kyrie*, *Gloria*, *Credo*, *Sanctus* and *Agnus Dei*) – or perhaps only the first three, as no *Sanctus* or *Agnus Dei* movements are found among the Turin MSS. A vespers setting comprised five psalms as prescribed for the day, a *magnificat* and possibly a hymn; the place of antiphons to the psalms seems to have been taken by motets and *introduzioni*. Quantz describes the Italian motet of the eighteenth century as 'a sacred cantata to Latin words consisting of two arias and two recitatives and closing with an *Alleluia*, sung during Mass after the Credo'.[1] A special class of motet, the *introduzione*, was sometimes used as a prefatory movement to a psalm or mass section.

We do not know which, if any, of the nearly fifty sacred compositions by Vivaldi in Turin are the ones referred to in the memorandum of the Pietà's governors dated 2 June 1715 (see p. 18), but some sparse stylistic and bibliographical clues suggest that the *Gloria* in D RV 588 (not RV 589, the well-known *Gloria* in the same key) and the *Credo* in E minor RV 591 are a fragment of the mass. As the Pietà

---

[1] Mozart's *Exsultate, jubilate* (K165), composed in 1773 for Milan, is a late representative of the genre.

was dedicated to the Virgin, it is quite natural that most of the psalms and many of the hymns belong to the liturgy of the Blessed Virgin Mary, although some important non-Marian festivals including Easter and Christmas as well as the feasts of certain saints such as St Lawrence the Martyr and St Anthony of Padua were also celebrated with appropriate music, instrumental and vocal.

It is likely that Vivaldi continued to supply the Pietà with sacred vocal music until 26 February 1719, when C. P. Grua was appointed as *Maestro di coro*. Two oratorios are known to have been written by him for the Pietà during this period: *Moyses Deus Pharaonis* (1714), of which only the libretto has survived, and *Juditha triumphans* (1716), preserved complete except for its introductory sinfonia.

In the interval between Grua's death (29 March 1726) and the appointment of his successor Giovanni Porta on 24 May 1726 Vivaldi may well have provided music for Holy Week and Easter. Another period when his services may have been required again was the interregnum between Porta's departure for Bavaria (September 1737) and the appointment of A. Gennaro (21 August 1739). One cannot entirely rule out the possibility that Vivaldi wrote sacred vocal music for the Pietà during the time in office of these successive *maestri di coro*, but it is difficult to imagine the circumstances in which they would have willingly ceded this privilege to a subordinate.

Further small clues to the dating of some of the works are provided by the appearance on four of the Turin scores, and on an example of the *Moyses* libretto in the S. Cecilia Conservatoire of Rome, of names of the girl soloists. Checking these names against the Pietà's records and a few other references, which include an amusing poem written around 1735, gives some very rough dates. The *Lauda Jerusalem* for double choir and orchestra must have been sung, if not composed, in the late 1730s, as two of the four girls (Chiaretta, Fortunata, Giulietta and Margarita) are described as young in the poem. The final version (RV 611) of Vivaldi's much-reworked *Magnificat* in G minor must date from about five to ten years earlier, as two of the five solo singers named in the score are given an age of twenty or slightly over in the poem, while one (Apollonia) is already a veteran of over thirty. This *Lauda Jerusalem* establishes, incidentally, that Vivaldi wrote most of his works for double orchestra and (where appropriate) choir not for St Mark's, as some have rather naïvely supposed, but for the Pietà.

It cannot have been long before he received outside commissions for sacred music. Two such works, both lost, are known: an oratorio to an Italian text (*L'adorazione delli tre rè magi al bambino Gesù*) for Milan (1722) and a *Te Deum* performed on 19 September 1727 in Venice at the French ambassador's residence in celebration of the birth of twin daughters to Louis XV. A number of sacred works by Vivaldi, including a complete mass, are preserved in the library of Warsaw University. Perhaps these reached Poland via Saxony. At any rate, one of them, the sacred aria *Eja voces plausum date* (R V 647), is certainly a latish work, being a *contrafactum* of an aria found in *Orlando furioso* (1727) and *L'Atenaide* (1729). Several further works have been discovered in various Czech libraries. These may well have been commissioned by Vivaldi's Austro-Bohemian patrons – men like Counts Collalto, Morzin and Wrtby.[1]

In classifying Vivaldi's church music the first distinction to be drawn is that between settings of liturgical and non-liturgical texts. To the first category belong mass sections, psalms, canticles and hymns; to the second, motets, *introduzioni* and oratorios. The generally irregular structure of texts taken from the Vulgate and from the Mass predisposes the composer to a through-composed form; whatever unifying devices he uses (such as a ritornello) are imposed on the text 'from without'. Hymns, however, have a strophic construction which the composer can reproduce, as Vivaldi does in his *Gaude Mater* (R V 613). The *Stabat Mater* (R V 621), which in Vivaldi's setting is a hymn for the feast of the Seven Dolours of the Blessed Virgin Mary, comprising only the first ten verses of the sequence (the two Scarlattis and Pergolesi set the complete text), mixes strophic and non-strophic elements: the music of the opening three movements (corresponding to verses 1–4) is used again for verses 5–8, while verses 9 and 10, plus a final 'Amen', are set to new music. In contrast, the texts of oratorios and motets, and inevitably the musical forms employed, mirror those of operas and cantatas. Even their poetic imagery has a strong whiff of Arcadia, as one sees from the references to the gods Apollo and Mars, the Furies and *amoretti* (cupids) in the libretto of *Juditha triumphans*!

Next we must distinguish within the liturgical category between single-movement and multi-movement works. From the fact that

[1] Johann Joseph von Wrtby was the nobleman for whom Vivaldi composed the two surviving trios for lute, violin and bass (R V 82 and 85) and the chamber concerto for lute, two violins and bass (R V 93).

the same psalm (*Beatus vir*) can be set both as a single movement (RV 598, in B flat) and as a series of movements (RV 597, in C major) it appears that the choice depended on the degree of solemnity of the occasion and the resources available. The most elaborate of the multi-movement compositions is perhaps the *Gloria* RV 589, which has twelve numbers, well contrasted in key, scoring and character. However, the *Credo* RV 591, which uses no vocal soloists or obbligato instruments, is on a more modest scale, having only four movements.

The vocal forces required vary greatly. Some liturgical works adopt a 'motet' scoring for soprano or alto soloist with single or (in the unique case of RV 616, a *Salve regina* in C minor) double orchestra. Others are choral, in four or five parts, extracting soloists (if needed) from the ranks of sopranos and altos. The identity of the tenors and basses in performances at the Pietà has aroused much speculation. Choristers at St Mark's and the Pietà's male staff have been put forward as candidates, yet lists of the Pietà's singers often have the words 'tenor' and 'basso' against a girl's name in a context where the terms can hardly stand for instruments. It is not impossible that a few girls took tenor parts as they stood (Ambrosina, one of the soloists in RV 611, sang from the tenor clef!), while the 'basses' sang an octave higher than the notated pitch. Where the organ and the various instruments on the bass line remained at the proper pitch, the effect would not have been unsatisfactory.

The role of the instruments is even more variable. Only one work, a *Credidi a 5* (RV 605), is from start to finish 'a cappella' (which in eighteenth-century usage means without independent instrumental parts rather than altogether without instruments). Perhaps significantly, this is not an original composition, being a *contrafactum* of an anonymous *Lauda Jerusalem* (RV Anh. 35) among the nineteen non-Vivaldian works, mostly unattributed, contained in the four volumes of sacred music in Turin. Vivaldi's only contribution was to add specifications for instrumental doubling. In this style of writing the two violins sometimes double soprano and alto straightforwardly, but Vivaldi often prefers (as in RV 605) to have the first violins double the altos at the octave above, leaving the second violins to play with the sopranos; this arrangement places the violins in a more natural register and lends an attractive sheen to the sound. Individual 'a cappella' movements or sections are found in many works – for example, in the openings of the *Magnificat* (RV 610, 610a and 611) and the *Kyrie* in G minor (RV 587), and in the 'Et incarnatus' of the

*Credo* (RV 591), all of which are based on common thematic material. The *Crucifixus* of RV 591 adds an interesting touch: crotchets in the vocal parts are often represented as quavers followed by a quaver rest in the corresponding instrumental parts; this heightens the sense of weary desolation already suggested by a curiously sparse texture.

Ex.20 RV 591 *(Credo a 4)*, 'Crucifixus', 19—22

(instrumental parts omitted)

In other places the strings, though independent to a large extent of the voices, remain wholly in the background. Their function in such cases is mainly one of sustaining a continuous texture, so that the voices can drop out and re-enter with maximum freedom. Without its instrumental backcloth the marvellously evocative 'Et in terra pax' of the earlier *Gloria* would be unable to unfold with such majestic unhurriedness.

Ex.21 RV 588 *(Gloria)*, 'Et in terra pax', 43—47

et in ter - ra

In most movements, however, the strings are at least part of the time not merely independent of the voices but at the centre of interest. When they are playing ritornellos or making short interjections, the problem of their combination with the voices hardly arises. When, on the other hand, they are kept going simultaneously with the voices, Vivaldi has to decide whether to compose the voices 'against' the instruments or vice versa. Often he takes the first course, but he also found – perhaps even invented – a new method of combination which became part of the central tradition of choral writing and is strongly evident in the 'Viennese' mass of the late eighteenth century. Its essence is simple: the voices present the main *themes*, whether homophonically or semi-contrapuntally, while the instruments (in particular the violins) constantly repeat characteristic short *figures* designed to be adaptable to any harmonic situation. Instead of foreground and background we have two complementary areas existing side by side. An excellent example of this treatment is the 'Et in terra pax' from the second *Gloria* (RV 589), where the violins weave patterns out of three motives formed respectively from crotchets, quavers and semiquavers, each occupying one bar. It is especially prevalent in works consisting of a single, long movement, for a repeated figuration in the instrumental parts is a good way of imparting the necessary degree of unity to a basically through-composed form. A pair of typical violin parts are seen in the following example. Observe how the general shape but not the exact intervallic structure of the motive is preserved in the exchanges between the violins.

Ex.22 RV 604 *(In exitu Israel)*, 64—66

A word needs to be said about Vivaldi's eight compositions for double choir and orchestra. None of them exploits the potentiality for thematic (in addition to merely spatial) contrast between the two ensembles, leaving us with the impression that Vivaldi was just not interested in polychoral writing as such. The primitive, single-choir version of the *Magnificat* (RV 610) was converted into a double-choir work (RV 610a) simply by the addition of cues on the score, and the three other works *in due cori* with which RV 610a is bibliographically, and therefore possibly also musically, linked – *Dixit Dominus* (RV 594), *Laudate pueri Dominum* (RV 603) and *Salve Regina* (RV 616) – do not possess any features which might dispel a suspicion that they are elaborations of single-choir works. As the second choir and orchestra independently contribute little beyond simple responses to the first choir and orchestra, it is possible that they were smaller ensembles or ones made up of less advanced players.

Vivaldi approaches the question of form in his sacred vocal music without prejudices. Discounting movements too brief to require a form to which one could attach a label, the vast majority of movements in the liturgical works are written in an *ad hoc* version of ritornello form. Where only a solo singer or pair of singers appears, the orchestra supplies the ritornellos and the singer(s) the episodes. In purely choral movements the lines of demarcation between ritornello and episode, though clearly discernible in thematic terms, do not correspond as neatly to the pattern of scoring, since the choir tends to sing without major pauses until almost the end of the movement, once it has made its entry following the initial ritornello. Single-movement works employing both chorus and soloists such as the *Beatus vir* (RV 598) and the *Lauda Jerusalem* are the most complex in form, since three, not two, basic scoring patterns have to be alternated.

A few movements are fugues in a traditional mould. Perhaps the most impressive of them in contrapuntal terms is the 'a cappella' fugue on two subjects forming the second 'Kyrie eleison' of RV 587. A short but very beautiful fugal 'Amen', in which the alto soloist to a large extent becomes just one part among several, ends the *Stabat Mater*. Ironically, Vivaldi's most celebrated choral fugue – the 'Cum sancto spiritu' ending the 'second' *Gloria* – is not in essence an original composition. Among the non-Vivaldian MSS in the Turin collection (all of which were possibly once owned by Vivaldi) is a *Gloria* dated 1708 by the minor Venetian composer G. M. Ruggieri. Vivaldi borrowed the finale for his 'first' *Gloria*, reducing its two choirs and orchestras to one and eliminating a second viola part. Where further differences occur, they seem to result from Vivaldi's desire to concentrate the movement and diminish the role of the instruments, which include a pair of oboes and a trumpet. For his 'second' *Gloria* Vivaldi made a fresh adaptation of Ruggieri's movement, this time increasing the prominence of the obbligato parts and making some improvements to the shape of the motives in some episodic sections.

To give some idea of how Vivaldi put together a large-scale choral work, various details of the movements in the well-known *Gloria* are tabulated opposite. It is fascinating to see how many echoes of RV 588 exist in RV 589, usually (but not always) at the same point in the text. One unusual feature of the earlier work was not imitated: RV 588 opens with an *introduzione* for alto (*Jubilate, o amoeni chori*, RV 639) dovetailed into the first movement of the *Gloria* proper.

By far the most important of Vivaldi's non-liturgical sacred works is *Juditha triumphans*, a masterpiece which deserves, like Verdi's *Requiem*, to become known as its composer's 'best opera'. It was obviously designed as a showpiece for the Pietà. The five principal roles (Juditha, Holofernes, Abra, Vagaus and Ozias) were tailor-made for the best singers, and the orchestra required reads almost like an inventory of the Pietà's instrumentarium: besides the usual strings Vivaldi uses two trumpets, timpani, two each of recorders, oboes and clarinets, a *salmoè*, five *viole all'inglese*, a viola d'amore, a mandolin, four theorboes (in two parts) and solo organ. No doubt

*Gloria in D, RV 589*

| Movement | Tempo | Key | Voices | Instruments[1] | Form |
|---|---|---|---|---|---|
| 1. Gloria in excelsis | *Allegro* | D | choir | strings, oboe, trumpet | ritornello |
| 2. Et in terra pax | *Andante* | b | choir | strings | ritornello |
| 3. Laudamus te | *Allegro* | G | 2 sopranos | strings | ritornello |
| 4. Gratias agimus tibi | *Adagio* | e | choir | strings (doubling) | unitary (chordal) |
| 5. Propter magnam gloriam | *Allegro* | e | choir | strings (doubling) | unitary (imitative) |
| 6. Domine Deus, rex caelestis | *Largo* | C | 1 soprano | solo violin or oboe | ritornello |
| 7. Domine fili unigenite | *Allegro* | F | choir | strings | ritornello |
| 8. Domine Deus, Agnus Dei | *Adagio* | d | 1 soprano/ choir | continuo/ strings (doubling) | ritornello |
| 9. Qui tollis | *Adagio* | e | choir | strings (doubling) | unitary (chordal) |
| 10. Qui sedes | *Allegro* | b | 1 alto | strings | ritornello |
| 11. Quoniam tu solus | *Allegro* | D | choir | strings, oboe, trumpet | ritornello (abridged No. 1) |
| 12. Cum Sancto Spiritu | *Allegro* | D | choir | strings, oboe, trumpet | fugue |

two players sufficed for all the woodwind instruments, since no more than one pair (recorders, oboes or clarinets) are heard together at any time. That Vivaldi meant clarinets by the parts designated 'claren' in the autograph score and not trumpets is established beyond doubt, but it is interesting to observe how closely the clarinets adhere to the trumpet style of writing at this early stage in the instrument's history.

*Juditha triumphans* contains twenty-one solo arias, two in alternative versions for the girl named Barbara who sang the part of Holofernes' henchman Vagaus (Begoas). The aptness of characterisation in them and their variety of expression are the equal of anything in the operas. Among the gems are a 'comparison' aria for Holofernes ('Agitata infido flatu') depicting the flight of a swallow buffeted by a howling wind, an aria for Juditha ('Veni, veni me sequere') to the seductive strains of the *salmoè*, which in evoking the turtle-dove anticipates this bird's appearance with a similar call in the 'Summer' concerto, and Vagaus' aria 'Armatae face' calling upon

[1] Continuo is naturally understood.

the Furies of Greek (!) mythology to avenge the murder of the Assyrian leader, a 'fury' aria if ever there was one.

The chorus is treated a little more generously than in Vivaldi's operas, though it still does not begin to approach in importance the chorus in Handel's oratorios. If this is to be counted a deficiency, the blame must rest with the librettist, Giacomo Cassetti, who writes for the chorus, which represents Assyrian warriors and Bethulian maidens in turn, as onlookers rather than protagonists.

The recitatives, which include *accompagnati* for Juditha and Ozias (in the Apocrypha a governor of Bethulia but here a high priest!), are finely wrought. Vagaus' discovery of his beheaded lord in the tent where he had supposedly spent a night of love-making with Juditha is memorably represented by a slowly ascending sequence (Vagaus' hesitant approach at dawnbreak to the tent), a brutal harmonic transition (his gasp at the sight of blood everywhere) and almost immediately another riveting progression (the sight of a decapitated Holofernes). Passages like this utterly belie the popular view of baroque recitative as a necessary evil.

It is gratifying to see that Vivaldi's dozen solo motets – if not yet his slightly less numerous *introduzioni* – are beginning to enter the concert repertoire, for they fill a niche not fully catered for by his French and German contemporaries.[1] All of them deviate from Quantz's formula in omitting the introductory recitative, a step analogous to the omission of an introductory slow movement in the concerto. They emphasise bravura rather than counterpoint or thematic development, but do so in such a sparkling manner that the loss is not felt. In the 'Alleluia' finales long melismas on the first syllable allow Vivaldi to shape his vocal line with the freedom of an instrumental composition – Ex. 23 opposite.

Yet while soaring and diving, scurrying and pausing, the voice is never forced into unnatural utterances. Vivaldi amply justifies Mattheson's high opinion of his vocal writing.

## *Vivaldi's Style*

In their attempts to assess and describe Vivaldi's influence on other

[1] J. S. Bach's cantata *Jauchzet Gott in allen Landen* (BWV 51) comes close in conception to the Italian motet.

Ex.23 RV 626 *(In furore)*, 'Alleluia', 1—8
(Soprano only)

composers historians have commonly laid emphasis on particular aspects of his music such as the form of his concerto movements and the character of his writing for the violin. Important though these are to the historian, they may strike the ordinary music-lover as less fundamental to the appreciation of Vivaldi's music than those aspects which reveal him as a composer with a unique vision. It is fitting to end this study with a look at some of the stylistic features which contribute to this uniqueness.

No composer in musical history has treated the sixth and seventh degrees of the minor scale with a flexibility to equal Vivaldi's. Each of the two forms of the 'melodic' minor scale – one with both sixth and seventh degrees lowered, the other with both raised – is used in contexts where standard practice prefers the alternative form. In Ex. 21 (see p. 93) the B minor tonic chord is twice alternated with a dominant chord in which the third is minor before a dominant chord with the expected major third (A sharp) arrives. Ex. 24 is even more striking, as the lowered sixth and seventh degrees (G and A natural) form part of an ascending tetrachord. Vivaldi also used the 'harmonic' minor scale (with lowered sixth and raised seventh degrees) melodically, in contexts where his contemporaries would have avoided the augmented second, perhaps by inverting the interval to make a diminished seventh (see the last bar of Ex. 24, second violin part).

**Ex.24** RV 124 (Op. 12 no. 3), 1st mvt, 41—43

He treats the third and fourth degrees of both major and minor scales in similarly flexible fashion. The minor scale sometimes has both notes raised in progressions ascending to the dominant, while in a major scale the use of a raised fourth (as in the finale of the *Concerto alla rustica* RV 151) often suggests the 'Polish' style, which both Telemann and Bach occasionally cultivated. Not infrequently, raised and lowered forms of the fourth (or seventh) degrees are sounded simultaneously (see Ex. 28, p. 103) producing an unusually acrid effect.

Passing to Vivaldi's use of melodic intervals, one can make another bold claim: he was the first composer to exploit the distinctive expressive potentiality of compound intervals (those greater than an octave) and even more of the octave itself. How many of his most memorable themes (e.g. the opening theme of the *Gloria* RV 589, or of the fifth concerto in Op. 3) open with a series of octave leaps interspersed with note-repetitions! And how commonplace the opening of the *Concerto funebre* would sound if, by removal of the octave displacements, its ninths became seconds (Ex. 25)!

In a recent book Walter Kolneder, the German scholar who, after

**Ex.25** RV 579 *(Concerto funebre)*, 1st mvt, 1—3

Pincherle, has done most to popularise Vivaldi's music, lends the apt term 'cadential melody' to a noteworthy feature of Vivaldi's melodic writing, particularly in his instrumental works. It refers to his habit of piecing together melodies from a series of short phrases, each of which outlines a cadential formula. Other Italian composers of the late Baroque, notably Domenico Scarlatti, share this method. What distinguishes Vivaldi's 'cadential' melodies is the copious use they made of fourths, fifths and octaves – intervals normally associated with bass rather than upper parts. In choosing to invest his melodies with something of the character of a bass Vivaldi may have been influenced by his experience of *unisono* writing, which he had done so much to foster in his early works.

His rhythms often have the flavour of folk music. The unusual anapaestic group ♪♪ ♩ and the syncopated group ♪ ♩ ♪ (or ♪ ♩ ♫), which are featured so prominently in many of his principal themes, suggest Slavic (Dalmatian or Bohemian?) influence. 'Lombardic' rhythms, with whose introduction Quantz credited Vivaldi, may have a native Italian origin. But could any composer have used them as relentlessly as Vivaldi in the following example?

**Ex.26** RV 714 *(La fida ninfa*, Verona, 1732), I/6, 'Aure lievi che spirate', 1—12 (violin part only, original notation)

His phrase-structure is even more remarkable. In the baroque period as today the division of a period or phrase into smaller units is usually *binary* (on the statement-response pattern) and at the lowest levels of organisation exact metrical symmetry is commonly sought. Vivaldi, however, often introduces a strong *ternary* element, either by pairing phrases of one and a half times the standard length or by grouping in threes phrases of standard length. The first arrangement is seen at the opening of Ex. 18 (p. 79), the second in Ex. 26 above. More complex patterns are possible: the phrase-structure, expressed in numbers of bars, of Ex. 16 (pp. 76–7) is 2 + 3 + 2 + 2 + 3 + 3.

His harmony is notable for its admission of the *seventh*, when required, to the essential structure of the chord. The note forming the seventh no longer has to be prepared in the previous chord or approached from another note of the same chord, as we still find in Bach and Handel. In Ex. 27 the sevenths (asterisked) in the violin part are approached conjunctly but otherwise receive no special treatment. Each seventh in the violin and viola parts is resolved in very oblique fashion onto the seventh of the next chord.

Ex.27 RV 628 *(Invicti bellate)*, 'Alleluia', 9–13

Vivaldi does not often admit the seventh to the dominant chord at cadences; this was more usual among French and German composers of the time. However, he makes a highly individual use of the leading-note chord strengthened with a minor or diminished seventh, treating it as the equivalent of a dominant chord. He frequently emerges from a sequence involving seventh chords in what may appear disconcertingly brusque fashion with a VII⁷-I cadence of this kind. Ex. 28 opposite, remarkable for other reasons besides, exemplifies this favourite progression. The viola's *f♮'* should be regarded as the bass (and root) of the chord, since the viola part is here functioning as a *bassetto*, or 'high' bass.

Not content with emancipating the seventh chord, Vivaldi pioneered the use of the *ninth* as a harmony note. Three different ways in which he employed it are seen in Ex. 15 (bar 19), Ex. 16 (bar 20) and Ex. 28. What these examples have in common is their refusal to treat the note at the ninth as an appoggiatura or suspension requiring resolution to the octave. On occasion, he even introduces as a harmony note the dominant *eleventh*, a third above the ninth!

Ex.28 RV 644 (*Juditha triumphans*), 'Agitata infido flatu', 17—18

(**Allegro**)

mae - sta  hi - run - du,___  mae - sta  hi - run - du

(*Trans.* 'The sad swallow (goes weeping)')

Through chromatic alteration of the appropriate notes Vivaldi arrived at many of the 'exotic' chords familiar to any advanced student of harmony – the chord of the 'Neapolitan' Sixth and the three chords of the Augmented Sixth, for example. These chords as such were well known to his contemporaries, some of whom like Caldara made less restrained use of them. Where Vivaldi scores is in the exciting, unforeseen contexts in which they are introduced. In the 'Et in terra pax' of the *Gloria* RV 589 a bass F natural in bar 64 supporting a seventh chord whose root is G is interpreted as its enharmonic equivalent E sharp, root of a 'German' Sixth chord, for the ensuing resolution onto an F sharp chord. To equate the dominant seventh with the 'German' sixth is a piece of harmonic sophistication a good fifty years ahead of its time!

Another harmonic 'vivaldism' is the admission of dissonances such as the fourth to broken-chord figures, so that when the upper parts arpeggiate a chord in similar motion the dissonance travels from part to part, and sometimes from octave to octave. Vivaldi is always scrupulous, however, in his resolution of the dissonance in each individual part.

There is one resource so extraordinary that conventional harmonic vocabulary cannot describe it. This is Vivaldi's practice of 'contaminating' a chord with one or more notes borrowed from the succeeding chord, as if to urge the progression forward. There is no way in which the first *e″* in the only complete bar of Ex. 29 overleaf (a note altered to *d″* in Bach's transcription!) can be explained otherwise. An engraving error is out of the question, as similar cases occur throughout Vivaldi's music.

Vivaldi's bass parts tend to be simpler than his upper parts. There are times, particularly in the solo episodes of his later concertos,

Ex.29 RV 565 (Op. 3 no. 11), 3rd mvt, 3—4

and in his violin sonatas, when the bass appears to be doing little other than maintaining a pulse by marking the principal beats. At other times, the bass moves dangerously in similar motion to the upper parts, courting the charge of parallel fifths or octaves. Since the venerated Corelli had once fallen foul of some theorists on this very score, we need not be too surprised that Quantz and Goldoni demurred at Vivaldi's basses. In all honesty one must admit that they had a point.

In the matter of harmonic rhythm (the pace of chord change) Vivaldi moves quickly and unpredictably from one extreme to the other. For bars on end he will dwell on one chord, suddenly to embark upon a dazzling succession of harmonies. If generalisation about his concerto movements is possible, the harmonic rhythm of his ritornellos tends to become more urgent as the movement progresses, aided by pruning which may halve or even quarter the length of phrases, while the episodes relax into a slower harmonic rhythm. This is an idiosyncrasy not taken over by his imitators.

The myth of Vivaldi the anti-contrapuntist has already been challenged in connexion with his fugal writing. There is one device which he uses more widely and with greater panache even than imitation: ostinato. We are speaking here of literal ostinato, in which a short motive is repeated several times as it stands against the other parts. When the ostinato is in the bass part, as in ground bass movements, Vivaldi does not allow it to dissonate more freely against the upper parts than an ordinary bass part; but when an upper part has an ostinato it is sometimes granted the harmonic privileges of a pedal-note. Ex. 24 (p. 100) is instructive: the bass has a pedal-note, but the main harmonic clashes are generated by the prominent note B in the ostinato of the first violins.

Another sign of the expert contrapuntist is his skill at diversifying the rhythms of his parts. The slow movement of the 'Spring' concerto (see Ex. 12, p. 67) is a good instance. But then it is also true that Vivaldi takes homorhythm (note-against-note writing) to its limits, as in the opening of the 'Summer' concerto. Fortunately for us, he was consistent only in the clarity with which he resolved problems of composition in their specific context.

His part-writing is often unorthodox, as shown by the countless 'dropped' leading-notes. It can be clumsy or careless – corrections in his autograph manuscripts show that the avoidance of forbidden 'parallels' was not second nature to him – but it is rarely dull. Some of the originality of the sound in his orchestral music stems from his inventive use of wide spacing to lend power and bring subsidiary parts into prominence, and close spacing to bring intensity. His parts seem to have so much more space to move in than those of most of his contemporaries.

Perhaps the most original aspect of Vivaldi's style, and the one which repays closest attention, is his treatment of modulation. Any student of his concertos will quickly see that whereas the circle of closely-related keys visited in the course of the movement is exactly the same as for other composers, the order in which they are visited is often highly unusual. In major keys the mediant (minor) is often substituted for the dominant as the first new key-centre visited; in minor keys it is sometimes the subdominant which fulfils the same role. There are even several binary movements in minor keys (e.g. the opening movements of the violin sonata RV 760 and the cello sonata RV 42) whose first section is addressed to the subdominant. Naturally, Vivaldi also uses the more orthodox keys of the relative major and dominant for the same purpose in other movements.

Unusually for an Italian composer of his period (Scarlatti as ever excepted), Vivaldi in his later works moves with the greatest freedom between the major and minor keys sharing a tonic. Sometimes themes are heard first in one mode and then immediately in the other, in a manner prophetic of Mozart and Schubert – Ex. 30 overleaf.

Further-ranging modulations occur quite often in his music (not counting recitatives and short, bridging *adagio* movements, where they are, so to speak, endemic). In these modulations Vivaldi usually moves stage by stage through the circle of fifths, flatwards or sharpwards, although major-minor shifts of the sort just illustrated and even enharmonic changes are employed to effect more rapid or dramatic transitions.

Some of Vivaldi's modulations can seem over-abrupt on first

**Ex.30** RV 740 *(Il Tigrane)*, II/2, 'Mi vedrai con lieta fronte', 1–5
(Violin 1 only)

hearing. In his daemonic urge to forge ahead he often cut corners, establishing new keys with the minimum of preparation – or none at all. However, it often happens that on repeated hearing a suspect modulation begins to convince. As with Berlioz, a figure of comparable originality in the next century, a lot depends on whether the listener is 'on the composer's side' to start with or not.

Another parallel with Berlioz suggests an appropriate conclusion to this study, written for the tercentenary of Vivaldi's birth when the revaluation which such events bring about draws near. Both men wrote music which one must either admire greatly or not at all: affectionate respect is an attitude difficult to maintain in the face of so strong an artistic personality. Neither is likely ever to become a 'musician's musician' in the sense that Bach, Mozart and perhaps Stravinsky merit the term, if only because their works lack the final degree of technical and aesthetic perfection.

At this point we must put aside the parallel, for whereas Berlioz strove in his own fashion for perfection, as any self-respecting artist of his time was bound to do, Vivaldi had the more limited and less idealistic perspectives of an artisan, content with immediate success. This makes the frequency with which, through the quality of his inspiration, he was able to transcend the conditions under which he worked and his own mercenary intentions all the more remarkable.

It is fashionable today to decry the notion that great art is born of suffering. While conceding that suffering degrades as often as it ennobles, and distracts the mind as often as it concentrates it, one may still claim that in certain artists it acts as a beneficial catalyst in the creative process. Is it fanciful to discern behind the furious energy of Vivaldi's music the frustration of a man condemned from childhood to lead a sedentary life? Or to glimpse in some of the slow movements the doubts of a man outwardly so self-satisfied? This much is certain: no composer before the nineteenth century better deserves the epithet 'romantic', and no composer has written music of greater power and originality.

## Index to Vivaldi Works Cited

### 1. Instrumental Works

Column 1 identifies works by their number in Peter Ryom's *Verzeichnis der Werke Antonio Vivaldis* (Leipzig, 1974). This is a short version (*kleine Ausgabe*) of a larger catalogue in preparation. The numbers are given in ascending order (those from RV 760 onwards are late entries in the Ryom catalogue).

Column 2 gives the corresponding volume (*tomo*) number in the collected edition of Vivaldi's instrumental works (*Opere Strumentali*) published from 1947 onwards by Ricordi.

Column 3 gives the Pincherle numbers as published in the *Inventaire Thématique*, second volume of Marc Pincherle's *Antonio Vivaldi et la Musique Instrumentale* (Paris, 1948). For sonatas Pincherle does not provide numbers as such, but the works can be located in his catalogue by a combination of page number and position on the page (e.g., 6/2 denotes the second work on p. 6). Sinfonias form a separate series, whose numbers will be prefaced by the letter S. The primary series, for concertos, has no prefatory letter (other than P. for Pincherle).

Column 4 indicates on which pages of the present book reference is made to each work. The use of italics denotes the presence of a musical illustration.

| RV | OS | P. | pages |
|----|-----|------|------|
| 3 | 366 | 6/2 | 66n |
| 6 | 372 | 5/5 | 66n |
| 10 | 364 | 5/10 | 68 |
| 12 | 365 | 6/1 | 66n |
| 16 | 402 | 2/9 | *67* |

| RV | OS | P. | pages |
|---|---|---|---|
| 25 | 371 | 5/4 | 68 |
| 26 | 373 | 5/6 | 68 |
| 31 | 395 | 2/2 | 67 |
| 41 | 474 | 4/6 | *69* |
| 42 | 530 | — | 105 |
| 53 | 375 | 6/3 | *70–1* |
| 59 | 470 | 4/2 | 66n |
| 63 | 393 | 1/12 | 63 |
| 71 | 17 | 7/5 | *65* |
| 79 | 392 | 1/11 | 63 |
| 82 | 63 | 7/3 | 90n |
| 83 | 20 | 7/1 | 66 |
| 85 | 75 | 7/2 | 90n |
| 86 | 18 | 7/8 | 66 |
| 90 | 42 | 155 | 54 |
| 93 | 62 | 209 | 59, 90n |
| 95 | 154 | 204 | 53 |
| 106 | 41 | 404 | 60 |
| 107 | 40 | 360 | 59–60 |
| 110 | 200 | 61 | 40n |
| 114 | 493 | 27 | 59 |
| 124 | 464 | 157 | 23n, *57–9, 99–100* |
| 129 | 36 | 86 | 36 |
| 130 | 21 | 441 | 57n, 60 |
| 133 | 492 | 113 | 59 |
| 144 | 512 | 145 | 59 |
| 151 | 49 | 143 | 53, 100 |
| 163 | 9 | 410 | *39* |
| 169 | 22 | S.21 | 57n |
| 172 | 322 | 19 | 45 |
| 180 | 81 | 7 | 53 |
| 206 | 497 | 177 | 40n |
| 208 | 314 | — | 30 |
| 209 | 286 | 193 | *50* |
| 210 | 84 | 153 | 45 |
| 230 | 414 | 147 | 30, *32* |
| 237 | 325 | 277 | *47* |
| 243 | 45 | 310 | 49 |
| 249 | 425 | 253 | 44 |

| RV | OS | P. | pages |
|-----|-----|-----|-------|
| 253 | 80 | 415 | 86 |
| 265 | 417 | 240 | 30 |
| 269 | 76 | 241 | *54–5*, 86 |
| 270 | 15 | 248 | 47n |
| 271 | 297 | 246 | 53 |
| 293 | 78 | 257 | 54 |
| 299 | 449 | 102 | 30 |
| 310 | 408 | 96 | 30, 48 |
| 315 | 77 | 336 | 104–5 |
| 316 | — | — | 30, 31 |
| 334 | 127 | 339 | 48n |
| 343 | 100 | 229 | 49 |
| 348 | 129 | 215 | 49 |
| 356 | 411 | 1 | 46 |
| 381 | 514 | 327 | 30 |
| 391 | 125 | 154 | *49–50* |
| 428 | 456 | 155 | 54 |
| 442 | 46 | 262 | 86 |
| 443 | 105 | 79 | *43* |
| 447 | 216 | 41 | 45 |
| 455 | 14 | 306 | 52, 70 |
| 460 | 127 | 339 | 48n |
| 496 | 214 | 381 | 52 |
| 502 | 270 | 382 | 52 |
| 519 | 410 | 212 | 100 |
| 522 | 413 | 2 | 30, 45, 47 |
| 540 | 320 | 266 | 56 |
| 541 | 95 | 311 | 56 |
| 542 | 353 | 274 | 56 |
| 543 | 265 | 301 | 56 |
| 544 | 135 | 308 | 56 |
| 545 | 280 | 129 | 56 |
| 546 | 146 | 238 | 56 |
| 547 | 35 | 388 | 56 |
| 548 | 73 | 406 | 56 |
| 556 | 54 | 84 | 56–7 |
| 558 | 318 | 16 | 56 |
| 559 | 10 | 74 | 56–7 |
| 560 | 3 | 73 | 56–7 |

| RV | OS | P. | pages |
|----|-----|------|------------------------|
| 565 | 416 | 250 | 30, 44, 45, *103–4* |
| 579 | 51 | 385 | 86, *100–1* |
| 580 | 415 | 148 | 30, *31* |
| 581 | 55 | 14 | 57 |
| 582 | 141 | 164 | 57 |
| 583 | 136 | 368 | 49 |
| 760 | — | — | 105 |
| 763 | — | — | 48–9, *51*, 53 |
| 766 | — | — | 56 |
| 767 | — | — | 56 |
| Anh. 65 | 485 | 217 | 23n |

## 2. *Vocal Works*

In this section of the Index Ryom numbers appear, as before, in Column 1. Column 2 gives the title or text incipit as appropriate of each work. Page references appear in Column 3.

| RV | description | pages |
|--------|------------------------------|-----------------------------------|
| 587 | *Kyrie* | 36, 91–2, 96 |
| 588 | *Gloria* | 88, *92–4*, 96 |
| 589 | *Gloria* | 34, 88, 94, 96, 97, 100, 103 |
| 591 | *Credo* | 88, 91, *91–2* |
| 594 | *Dixit Dominus* | 95 |
| 597 | *Beatus vir* | 90–1 |
| 598 | *Beatus vir* | 90–1, 95–6 |
| 603 | *Laudate pueri Dominum* | 95 |
| 604 | *In exitu Israel* | *85* |
| 605 | *Credidi* | 91 |
| 609 | *Lauda Jerusalem* | 89, 95–6 |
| 610–11 | *Magnificat* | 36, 89, 91–2, 95 |
| 613 | *Gaude Mater* | 90 |
| 616 | *Salve regina* | 91, 95 |
| 621 | *Stabat Mater* | 34, 90, 96 |
| 622 | *Te Deum* | 90 |
| 626 | 'In furore' | *99* |
| 628 | 'Invicti bellate' | *102* |
| 639 | 'Jubilate, o amoeni chori' | 96 |
| 643 | *Moyses Deus Pharaonis* | 18, 89 |